T0139200

Patient-Focused Network Integration in BioPharma

Strategic Imperatives for the Years Ahead

Patient-Focused Network Integration in BioPharma

Strategic Imperatives for the Years Ahead

Rob Handfield, PhD

CRC Press
Taylor & Francis Group
Boca Raton   London   New York

CRC Press is an imprint of the
Taylor & Francis Group, an **informa** business

CRC Press
Taylor & Francis Group
6000 Broken Sound Parkway NW, Suite 300
Boca Raton, FL 33487-2742

© 2013 by Taylor & Francis Group, LLC
CRC Press is an imprint of Taylor & Francis Group, an Informa business

No claim to original U.S. Government works

Printed on acid-free paper
Version Date: 20130429

International Standard Book Number-13: 978-1-4665-5546-4 (Hardback)

Library of Congress Cataloging-in-Publication Data

Handfield, Robert B.
    Patient-focused network integration in biopharma : strategic imperatives for the years ahead / author, Rob Handfield.
        pages cm
    Includes bibliographical references and index.
    ISBN 978-1-4665-5546-4 (hardback)
    1. Pharmaceutical biotechnology. 2. Pharmaceutical biotechnology industry. 3. Biological products--Therapeutic use. 4. Communication in pharmacy. I. Title.

RS380.H37 2013
338.4'76151--dc23   2013013392

Visit the Taylor & Francis Web site at
http://www.taylorandfrancis.com

and the CRC Press Web site at
http://www.crcpress.com

Contents

Preface

This book started out as an interesting set of conversations with some very insightful and intelligent people. For twenty-five years I've studied supply chains in almost every industry, including oil and gas, automotive, electronics, industrial production, and even financial services. And every time I met with executives, I heard the same statement: "We're different—you don't understand." But in the end, after spending enough time with these executives, it became clear that the same principles of supply chain management applied. Perhaps a different context, different terminology, but in the end, the same rules applied.

When I started dabbling in healthcare, I originally encountered the same sets of objections. "Healthcare is different," I would hear, "After all, you have to consider the patient." But as I spent more and more time with healthcare executives, I only rarely heard the patient mentioned in the discussion. More often than not, the discussion focused on *compliance, reimbursement, diagnosis-related groups* (DRGs), and other terms that had very little to do with patient care. And as I studied the industry more, it became clear that organizations in the healthcare value chain, from the patient through hospitals, wholesalers, through insurance payers, manufacturers, and finally research and development (R&D), were not very well connected at all. In fact, they each seemed to be operating independently, and the patient was often the very last parameter mentioned in the debate.

This led me to engage in a series of research projects, the culmination of which are the seven chapters in this book. Each chapter can be read as a stand-alone piece of research. However, the common theme throughout the book is that of the need for a life sciences network evolution. This is depicted as a common thread—the *healthcare supply chain maturity model*, which is described in the second chapter of the book. The book explores the proposition that in order to sustain itself, parties in the healthcare network will need to coevolve, and form a more fluid and streamlined approach to healthcare that is focused primarily on the patient. This proposition is further supported by extensive research I've conducted over the last five years through executive interviews, surveys, focus groups, and multiagent simulations. Together, I hope they provide a set of insights to help guide executives toward a sustainable healthcare network.

Acknowledgments

There are several people who are worth mentioning, who were not only instrumental to this research, but highly supportive and directly contributed to the insights contained in this book. They include Christian Rosetti, Bill Welch, and Dick Kouri from North Carolina State University; Robert Lechich from Pfizer; Brian Daleiden at Tracelink; Steve Day and Phil Priest of GSK; Lou Arp from Eisai; Joydeep Ganguly, Karen Arnold, Rob Ciamarra, and Ben Matthews from BiogenIdec; Allen Esses from DataPros; Tom Nash and Dr. Tom Fasciewski from Ministry Healthcare; Gene Schneller from Arizona State University; Josh Feldstein from CAVA; and countless others. I also want to thank North Carolina State University for granting me the sabbatical that allowed me to actually sit down and finish compiling the book. Of course, many thanks to my wife Sandra, for her support, as always.

About the Author

Rob Handfield is the Bank of America University Distinguished Professor of Supply Chain Management at North Carolina State University and director of the Supply Chain Resource Cooperative (SCRC; http://scm.ncsu.edu). He earned his PhD in operations management from the University of North Carolina at Chapel Hill and a BSc in statistics from the University of British Columbia.

The SCRC is the first major industry–university partnership to include student projects in the MBA classroom in an integrative fashion, and has had seventeen major Fortune 500 companies participating as industry partners since 1999. Prior to this role, Handfield was an associate professor and research associate with the Global Procurement and Supply Chain Benchmarking Initiative at Michigan State University from 1992 through 1999, working closely with Professor Robert Monczka.

Handfield is the author of several books on supply chain management and healthcare, and has published many scholarly articles on the subject. He is considered a thought leader in the field of strategic sourcing, health-care supply chains, supply market intelligence, and supplier relationship management. He has spoken on these subjects across the globe, including China, Azerbaijan, Turkey, Latin America, Europe, Korea, Japan, Canada, and other venues.

1

Patient-Focused Network Integration in the Life Sciences

The biopharmaceutical and healthcare industry as we know it today is going through a massive change that is sending shudders to the massive onslaught of baby boomers entering retirement and what lies ahead. The reason for this change has its origins in the past sins of the industry to some extent, but also in the macroeconomic factors associated with the global economy and political regulation of the industry. This book argues that one of the key foci of executives in the life sciences and in healthcare needs to be on network integration. Very simply, all parties in the healthcare value chain network must align their strategic plans to derive innovation solutions. It is only through true collaboration and innovative aligned thinking that the parties in the drug development, distribution, payer, and provider network can deal with the incredible complexity and massive challenges that face the ecosystem.

Our thesis is that patient-focused network integration is the only path for the life sciences industry to evolve and thrive. For years, enterprises in the life sciences have focused on negotiating and contracting with their immediate supply chain partners upstream or downstream. Wholesalers negotiated with hospitals and group purchasing organizations, manufacturers with whole-salers, contract manufacturers with big pharmaceutical manufacturers, clinical trials with contract research organizations—and the list goes on and on. The missing element in all of these discussions has been the patient.

Patient-centric network integration is a new concept to these entities. It is a complex approach, that requires working with other parties who deliver and administer medicines to patients, not just the developers and manufacturers of the medicine. It also requires thinking beyond the immediate tier above or below your position in the supply chain.

Pulling together enterprises that seek to align objectives across the extended supply chain to drive operational improvement, innovation, joint outcomes, and aligned performance metrics is *critical*. If the patient is not the focal point of these metrics and outcomes, there is little chance that the industry can overcome the infrastructural barriers that have been constructed over thirty years of business relationships between payers, providers, and producers, who have focused solely on negotiating with one another. To these organizations, the notion of change, pay for performance, and personalized medicine is a frightening concept indeed.

INTRODUCTION: AN INDUSTRY IN FLUX

This book was developed over an eight-year period, based on interviews, conference presentations, one-on-one discussions, and review of multiple research papers, presentations, books, and articles. We met with hundreds of executives from biopharmaceutical manufacturers, insurance companies, and healthcare providers. We sought to obtain clear perspectives from multiple parties in the chain, including manufacturers, group purchasing organizations, retail pharmacies, hospital pharmacies, physicians, consultants, academics, clinical researchers, third-party logistics providers, pharmacy benefits managers, and others. Over the eight years, the level of anxiety has been mounting considerably, culminating with the angry response to President Obama's healthcare act in 2010, and the ensuing set of debates and political posturing that is taking place today in 2013.

The leader of the United States is facing a difficult road ahead. Although there are certainly flaws in the Obama healthcare legislation, this book is not going to take on the task of enumerating these flaws, nor is it our intent to encourage repeal of the Healthcare Reform Act. The objective here is to understand the historical context of the life sciences value chain, describe the current set of challenges facing the industry, and establish the agenda for change that lies ahead. Moreover, our position is that *Obamacare*, as many critics have named it, is really nothing more than a manifestation of what is happening globally in the healthcare ecosystem. There is a need for radical change, not so much in the provider policies, or the reimbursement process, or the drug approval process, but rather in the very elements of the value creation process that exists in the healthcare network. Current business models for the life sciences are not sustainable, and doing nothing in this case will serve only to allow patient care to suffer, costs to escalate, and drive the system to financial insolvency. This view is not just an opinion—a multiagent simulation model shows it to be the case.

A Multiagent Simulation View

The proposal that doing nothing to the current system will drive collapse has been validated by simulation findings, using multiagent-based simulation.* Using current models of biopharmaceutical development, the research suggests that the evolution of the current operating model, when carried out, results in complete insolvency and collapse.

A multiagent system involves interplay among multiple interacting agents. Although individual agents may follow a simple strategy, it may result in complex evolution of the system. Therefore, multiagent system (MAS) methodology can be used to analyze systems that are too complex to be solved using alternative methods (traditional mathematical or statistics). Application of MAS is ideal for problems whose solution is dynamic, uncertain, and of a distributed nature.

The research we carried out suggests that in the end, the current model of manufacturer consolidation (e.g., big pharma becoming bigger) is not effective (see Figure 1.1)

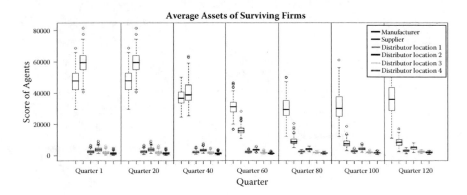

FIGURE 1.1
Multiagent simulation results.

* Guarav Jetly, Christian Rosetti, and Robert Handfield, "A Multi-Agent Simulation of the Pharmaceutical Supply Chain (PSC)," *Proceedings of the POMS 20th Annual Conference*, Orlando, FL, May 1–4, 2009. Baltimore: POMS, 2009.

According to our model, when manufacturers consolidate, they can't cover the cost of supporting their large asset base—plants, equipment, research laboratories, administration, and so on, as blockbusters begin to drop out of patent protection. Although their research productivity increases as they grow, as measured by the number of drugs released by individual manufacturers, the productivity of the supply chain diminishes. Drug sales represent a fixed pie, as only blockbusters will support the cash drain from larger assets. Because blockbusters are increasingly less likely to occur, it doesn't take a genius to determine where this ends up. The dramatic long-term results are shown in Figure 1.2.

In the simulation, merger activity is based on the acquirer's determination that the acquisition will perform above itself as well as above the industry average. As appears to be the case in reality, the agents assume that past performance in drug development is a good predictor of future performance. The acquirer examines each manufacturer based on the number of drugs it has released in the past two years. Unfortunately, by that time the drug is approaching its maximum sales. The larger manufacturer has a greater chance at creating a drug over many iterations. Results show that over the course of a sample of 177 iterations (e.g., cycles) however, the manufacturer is not assured that this increase in new drug development is greater than the number of drugs developed by large manufacturers.

Policy makers are tempted to regulate manufacturer prices in order to decrease their share of supply chain profits and pass savings on to consumers. Our findings show that this form of regulation may have a limited impact. Currently, manufacturers are spending in excess of 20% of

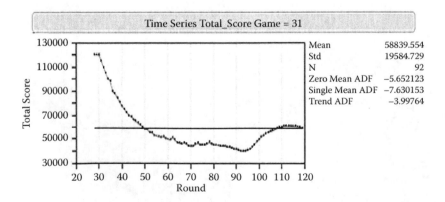

FIGURE 1.2
Results: Supply chain performance over time.

their revenues on sales and marketing activities. This activity is deemed necessary to fulfill a requirement for blockbuster drugs. Our results suggest that blockbusters are more necessary than the number of drugs released. If prices are limited, manufacturers will more likely cut back on research and development activities and focus more energy on marketing.

In addition, the results found that distributors have a limited impact on supply chain profitability. Manufacturers and suppliers that released new drugs *and* continued to acquire new companies improved profitability. However, manufacturers who acquired new companies were not always more productive in terms of research productivity, which also reduced the overall combined level of profitability. Consolidation at the supplier level increased supply chain profitability because rents from increased bargaining power are passed on to consumers. Overall, however, the net value of these firms decreased to the point where larger companies ended up producing fewer new drugs for patients, and profits eroded.

A Blueprint for the Future

As this simulation shows, not only is the old operational model broken, but the rules of the game are changing as well. The very nature of the health-care industry is undergoing a rapid series of changes that are unprecedented in the industry. These seven fundamental shifts in the healthcare market portend major challenges ahead that are disrupting current modes of entry and growth in the industry. These are illustrated in Figure 1.3.

Growing Adoption of Price Restrictions by Regulators and Governments

This is a trend that is not just occurring within the United States, but throughout the world. Even though pharma and biologics constitute 10% of the healthcare bill in most countries, the pharma bill is an easy target because it is so concrete and can be directly influenced because it is a fixed price. In fact, research has found that administrative costs are responsible for between 20% and 30% of U.S. healthcare spending.[*] Hospital spending accounts for nearly 33% of all expenditure, and prescription products for just 10.1%. Governments focus on pharmaceuticals, often because of

---

[*] Anna Bernasek, "Health Care Problem? Check the American Psyche," *New York Times*, December 31, 2006.

KEY ISSUES FACING THE INDUSTRY	PHARMA R&D & MFG	PHARMA DISTRIBUTORS	PAYERS (GOVERNMENT, REGULATORS)
1. Growing adoption of price restrictions by regulators and governments	Reduced margins to drive R&D budgets	Margin pressure passed on by payers	Ability to drive patients to lower cost medications
2. Declining R&D Productivity	Fewer blockbusters, move to acquire biologics	Transition to generics and biologics channels	Increasing drugs going to generics, lower costs overall
3. Increasing emphasis on personalized medicine and pay for performance	Biomarkers and testing protocol	Fragmented distribution channels	Increased pressure for patient outcome-based payments
4. Fragmentation of global mass markets	Smaller target populations	Higher channel costs	Increasing array of global payment schemes
5. Emergence of biotech and biological treatments as predominant growth markets	Shift away from tablets	Increased cold chain requirements	Increased cost of treatment (thousands per year for a single drug)
6. Biosimilars and interchangeable biologics	Protection of IP	Increasing threat of counterfeit and greater serialization	Greater competition from biosimilars
7. More restrictive clinical evidence	Increasing cost of clinical trials	Growth in global markets but increasing complexity	Increased restrictions on payment based on evidence of patient outcomes
8. Increased use of pervasive monitoring	Customized therapies	Requirements for monitoring and patient compliance	Patient compliance drives reimbursements
9. Changing role of primary and secondary care	Injection technologies and devices important	Channel fragmentation	Complex reimbursement channels

FIGURE 1.3
Impact of industry trends on supply chain participants.

the public perception that the medicine bill is much higher than it really is. For example, a survey conducted by the PWC Health Research Institute found that 97% of consumers estimated that prescription medicine accounted for at least 15% of overall U.S. healthcare costs, but 63% put the figure between 40% and 79%.* These elements of healthcare (physician fees, overhead, etc.) are more slippery and difficult to measure, and thus more difficult to control. As we have seen, in many global regions such as the European Union (EU) and China, there is only *one* payer: the government. This increases negotiating leverage and is one reason why prices in the United States are higher than anywhere else in the world. This is going to change. The U.S. market is now under increasing pressure for price reductions, and "Obamacare" is only the first of many new forms of regulation that are coming down on the industry.

There is also recognition that the healthcare industry cannot operate in a vacuum. Although the regulatory agencies are an external force for compliance, they also need to be integrated into the thinking and solution development process. This includes not just the Federal Drug Administration (FDA), but government payers, insurance providers, the Department of Health and Human Services, state agencies, and other parties that are impacted in one way or another in the industry. By integrating these parties into collaborative discussions with private industry, there is a chance of an improved outcome as for the extended network that we call healthcare.

For example, in one situation we encountered, the establishment of a specification for a drug substance was established by a researcher in a separate location, which was *not* shared and *not* sourced in the system. Compliance with the agency proved to be difficult, to say the least! But organizations are often not aware of the requirements for accessing information later in the development of the drug cycle. There is a need for some standard processes that can be created with agencies to ensure that everyone knows where the information resides, how accessible it is, how will it be used in the regulatory process, and by whom.

Declining Research and Development (R&D) Productivity

It is no secret that the number of blockbusters has all but dried up. A core problem has been the lack of innovation in making effective new therapies

---

* PricewaterhouseCoopers Health Research Institute, *Recapturing the Vision: Restoring Trust in the Pharmaceutical Industry by Translating Expectations into Actions*, 2006. http://www.pwc.com/he_IL/il/publications/assets/11recapturing.pdf. Accessed March 22, 2013.

for the world's unmet medical needs. A second problem has been the increasing scrutiny of new medicines. The FDA has become more severe in its regulatory stance on "me-too" drugs that do not have measurably improved efficacy over existing drugs. Despite the record billions of spending on R&D, the number of new approved drugs has been paltry relative to the number of branded products going off patent. There is no doubt that pharma's R&D processes have become complex and cumbersome. However, the increased scrutiny has not helped. When they start developing a new medicine, researchers do not know whether it will be eligible for reimbursement, and in many countries they are not allowed to seek guidance from the relevant government agencies. Most of the money invested in R&D is going to line extensions and other work, as distinct from new development projects. The international laws governing intellectual property rights have compounded this problem. And to complicate the issue, the push to maximize the number of candidate molecules in Phase III of development, to improve analysts' valuation of the company, may incur extra costs. It may have been better to weed out some of these molecules at an earlier and cheaper stage of development. As a result, manufacturers will need to focus more on targeted therapies that will address the world's most critical diseases. For instance, the number of people in India with diabetes is projected to reach 73.5 million in 2025.[*] Fear about flu pandemics has driven more interest in vaccines, and preventive medicine is becoming an area of increasing support by governments. But oncology is by far the most significant new therapeutic area. According to IMS, there are ninety therapeutic vaccines for cancer in the pipeline, and many of the new diseases (including obesity, liver and pancreas disease, lung cancer, melanoma, and others) will require greater focus on preventive medicine, not just pills for ills. Healthcare payers will not just be negotiating prices, but will begin to stipulate best medical practices, and access to extensive amounts of outcome data will provide more ammunition.

Emphasis on Pay for Performance and Personalized Medicine

As we discussed earlier, the emphasis on pay for performance is a phenomenon that is here to stay. Several countries have set up agencies specifically to compare the safety and efficacy of different forms of intervention and promote the use of evidence-based medicine. These include the U.S. Agency

---

[*] IMS Institute for Informatics 2010.

for Healthcare Research and Quality, the UK Centre for Health Technology Evaluation, the Australian Pharmaceutical Benefits Advisory Committee, and the Finnish Office for Health Care Technology Assessment. In the United States and Europe, an electronic medical records network will be established by 2020, which will form the basis for evaluating the clinical and economic performance of many therapies. In this environment, healthcare policy makers and payers will use outcomes' data to determine best practice, and there is no doubt some medicines will not be passed. Second, the price any therapy can command will be based on its performance, not what the manufacturer thinks is a fair price. A value-based pricing system in which the prices of products are set by comparing their clinical value with that of other treatments for the same condition is likely.*

Pay for performance will continue to grow in application, not only by private health insurers but also by the Centers for Medicare and Medicaid. Many of these pay-for-performance schemes are targeted at biologics in particular, where the cost of these medicines is rising due to the focus on "orphan diseases."

One of the major impacts associated with the high cost of payment for biologics is also taking place in drug development.[†] The FDA recently approved for sale a new AstraZeneca PLC cardiovascular drug called ticagrelor that had the potential to be a blockbuster drug. But regulatory approval is just the first step; the second is getting insurance companies and government health systems to pay for the expensive new drug. AstraZeneca, negotiating with U.S. insurers over the coverage of tricagrelor (brand name Bilinta), is faced with slow approval for reimbursement. To do so means assembling whole teams to shower insurers with data that they hope will prove that their drugs are worth paying for. This means showing, in this case, that the drug prevents heart attacks, hospitalization, and other expensive problems. This is also extending back to the clinical trials phase, and relates to the problem of understanding how payers look at value. For instance, there is resistance to ticagrelor in Europe, where a rival drug, clopidogrel, is available as a low-cost generic. Both treatments are designed to prevent blood clots, which cause heart attacks, but the generic costs about 24 euros, versus 3.5 euros for ticagrelor. French health

* PricewaterhouseCoopers Health Research Institute, *Pharma 2020: The Vision. Which Path Will You Take?*, 2007.
† Jeanne Whalen, "Hurdles Multiply for Latest Drugs," *Wall St. Journal*, August 1, 2011. Pane B1. http://online.wsj.com/article/SB10001424053111904233404576459851152423110.htm. Accessed March 22, 2013.

authorities ruled there was "insufficient evidence" of ticagrelor's benefits over clopidogrel. In Germany, when a company launches a drug, it gets to set the price for the first year, and then a government-appointed committee reviews data and decides whether the drug provides additional benefit over an older treatment. If it does, a price is negotiated. If it doesn't, the new drug is priced at the level of the older drug.

This policy trend in Germany is likely to spread to other countries, including the United States, in the near future. Companies like AstraZeneca have established *payer excellence academies* to train sales and marketing staff about dealing with insurers and state healthcare systems. They are also signing deals with health insurers, such as Wellpoint, allowing it to analyze how its drugs have performed versus other treatments in the 36-million-patient base that Wellpoint serves. More of these types of studies will be required to justify the high cost of drugs in the future to regulators and payers.

As discussed earlier, the emphasis on personalized medicine will continue to grow. This will radically change the manner in which prescriptions for most primary-care medications will be fulfilled. As boundaries blur, patients will require more information about the medicine they take, more advice, education, and monitoring. This will profoundly change delivery of medicines to patients, and companies will need to provide a full range of products and services. Increasingly, diagnostics will be a much bigger part of the overall product offering, which is a function of personalized medicine. A foundational principle for personalized medicine is pharmacogenomics, the science that allows researchers to predict the probability of a drug response based on a person's genetic makeup. Mass-produced drugs for a one-size-fits-all market are a thing of the past; no longer will people take average doses, with adjustments made if the patient experiences side effects. The terms *personalized medicine* and *targeted therapies* imply that interventions will be for a specific disease or condition, based on an understanding of the relevant genetic variations among individuals with that disease. These differences among individuals will guide the use and interpretation of diagnostics, as well as choices in therapies and preventions. What this means, practically, for the industry, is that therapies will now be paid based on certain biomarkers being present. A biomarker could be an enzyme, a DNA sequence, or an RNA expression profile that defines a physiological space. For example, a biomarker for breast cancer is the expression of a particular protein called HER. Females who have an expression of HER in their breast cancer are at a high risk of death, because that tumor will metastasize, grow, and be lethal. Genentech designed a drug that is specifically targeted at HER, called Herceptin. Herceptin worked so well that the FDA did not conduct a Phase III clinical trial, but approved the product after Phase II. For these types of drugs, an indication of a certain condition will be the requirement for approval. Similarly, the presence of certain diagnostic evidence may disclose that the drug will *not* be effective, and will therefore not be approved for certain populations. We are in the early stages of this science, but this is a phenomenon that will grow more in the future.

Fragmentation of Mass Markets

It is no surprise that global markets have become the focus of many manufacturers. The expansion of supply chains will bring many complications, including the challenges of parallel trading and counterfeiting. In addition, the number of products companies make will increase, and the nature of packaging and regulatory requirements will fractionate many product lines for presentation into these different global markets, each with their peculiar regulatory requirements. Some have suggested that this will result more in an assemble-to-order production and distribution environment in the future, which may entail postponement strategies for late-stage packaging and customization in the global supply chain at remote locations and distribution centers.* This has indeed already begun, as many third-party contract manufacturers and third-party logistics providers have entered the global life sciences landscape. Unfortunately, there is a massive need for greater collaboration in an outsourced environment—something the traditional players have not done well in the past (as documented in this book). Strategic partners, close integration at all stages in the product life cycle, and support services tailored to the specific needs of personalized medicine will need to be developed. This will require a radical rethinking of current operating models.

Emergence of Biotech and Biologics

As we have noted earlier, biologics are an important emerging area of growth. For distribution, however, unique challenges are presented.

Biologics work by targeting specific parts of the body's immune system to combat inflammation. They have proven very effective at relieving

---

* PricewaterhouseCoopers Health Research Institute, *Pharma 2020: The Vision. Which Path Will You Take?*, 2007.

symptoms and helping people with ailments (such as Crohn's disease) achieve long-term remission. However, in part because the manufacturing process is more complex for biologics than for some other drugs, biologics have a steep price tag. Even people who have health insurance can spend a lot of money on biologics. Virtually all Medicare plans and some commercial health insurance plans put biologics in the fourth tier of their drug formularies. Rather than having a copayment, consumers must pay a percentage—typically 25% to 35% of the cost of drugs in this top tier.

This has led to an interesting debate on whether insurance companies will be willing to fund the higher cost of biologics. Some examples include the following:

- Recently approved biologic drug treatments for severe psoriasis cost more than the average annual house payment according to a recently published article (between $170,000 and $320,000) over a thirty-year period.*
- One year of maintenance treatment with biologics for Crohn's disease can add up to about $20,000.
- A recent study at the University of Toronto discovered that biologics are more effective than methotrexate in achieving a short-term response in juvenile idiopathic arthritis (JIA) patients with prior inadequate responses to disease-modifying antirheumatic drugs (DMARDs); JIA is the most common chronic pediatric rheumatic disease and can have long-term effects leading to disability in adulthood. The study population consisted of polyarticular-course JIA patients with a prior inadequate response or intolerance to DMARDs. However, this comes at a high annual cost, as the biologics in question are much more expensive than DMARDs, and treatments cost in excess of $26K–$44K more than the DMARDS. The study concluded that adequate long-term data with respect to both safety and effectiveness are not currently available, nor are utility estimates. Such data will be important to estimate value in money for treating JIA with biologic drugs over the long term.†

---

* National Biological, http://www.natbiocorp.com
† W. J. Ungar, V. Costa, R. Hancock-Howard, B. M. Feldman, and R. M. Laxer, "Cost-Effectiveness of Biologics in Polyarticular-Course Juvenile Idiopathic Arthritis Patients Unresponsive to Disease-Modifying Antirheumatic Drugs," *Arthritis Care Res* 63, no. 1 (2011): 111–119, http://www.ncbi.nlm.nih.gov/pubmed/20740607

Why are biologics so costly?* There are several reasons listed by researchers.

- **The cost of making them.** Biologic agents are more expensive to make than chemical drugs like DMARDs. The materials needed to create them cost more, and the manufacturing process, which uses live organisms, is more complex.
- **The cost of research and development.** Developed through technology called *genetic modification*, biologics target specific parts of the inflammatory process involved in rheumatoid arthritis (RA) while sparing others. Drug makers say the cost of researching and developing these drugs makes them much more expensive than chemical drugs.
- **Less brand competition.** Because many of the biologics work in different ways to reduce inflammation, they face less competition from similar drugs. As a result, pharmacy benefit managers aren't able to negotiate prices for biologics.
- **The way they are given.** Some of the biologics are infused in a rheumatologist's office or infusion center. By contrast, most traditional pharmaceutical drugs are taken by mouth at home. The fact that some biologics are infused also affects the way Medicare reimburses for them.
- **Lack of generics.** When a drug company applies for a patent, it has exclusive rights to make and market the drug during a certain period of time. After that time, other companies can make cheaper generics. All of the current biologics are still under patent protection.
- **Pay for performance.** Perhaps one of the most challenging elements in the regulatory environment for the biopharmaceutical supply chain is the increasing focus on pay for performance, which is being adopted by insurers and the Centers for Medicare and Medicaid. Many of these are being targeted at biologics in particular.

---

* B. Welch, "Adalimumab (Humira) for the Treatment of Rheumatoid Arthritis," *American Family Physician* 78, no. 12 (2008): 1406–1408; The Johns Hopkins Arthritis Center, "Rheumatoid Arthritis Treatment"; "Drug Guide: Biologics," Arthritis Today; Kaiser Health News: "Checking In with Patricia Danzon on the Hot Topic of 'Biologics,'" Kaiser Health News; David I. Weiss, MD, rheumatologist, Arthritis Associates, Hattiesburg, MS; Medicare.gov: "5 Ways to Lower Your Costs during the Coverage Gap," "Help with Medical and Drug Costs, 2008."

Biologics are particularly hard to manufacture and transport, because they are more fragile than small molecules and more susceptible to impurities in the manufacturing process. There may also be unique technologies for delivery, including controlled-release implants and magnetically targeted carriers. Cold chain requirements, requiring temperature-controlled distribution monitoring, is also challenging in a global environment. We will cover in greater detail some of the specific elements that may drive this in the future. With the merging toward a single network, it is also imperative that we no longer differentiate between solely *biopharma* or *pharma* interests. Biopharmaceuticals (biopharma) pertain to larger molecules only (i.e., biological products). Biopharma is concerned primarily with vaccines and biologicals (blood products, etc.). Pharma focuses on pills (solid single-dose tablet formulations, etc). Vaccines are tied to a real-world updating of what is happening from a medical perspective. Acetaminophen (small molecule) is a standard small model.

To truly drive innovation and change in the life sciences, it is therefore imperative that we think of the entire spectrum of pharma, biologics, and vaccines. There are several reasons for this.

First, more companies are utilizing solutions that span both small- and large-molecule solutions. Many companies with a large-molecule historical focus (e.g., GSK, Pfizer, AstraZeneca, Merck, Roche) are being drawn more into the small-molecule space, which has been dominated by start-up firms that grew quickly (e.g., Genzymes, BiogenIdec, Genentech, and others).

But there are also technical reasons for thinking about the merging of these boundaries. In the example of a glass dual-syringe project with a chief marketing officer (CMO) working with a large pharmaceutical company, executives were primarily focused on the drug product side of the business, and have been for a long time. However, what is learned and used with drug product may also be applied to a different set of parameters. It is important to know that, because if one is working with active pharmaceutical ingredients (APIs) or drug substances, for example, the lessons learned and applications can apply the same methodologies and techniques. One example cited is sterilization, which spans from process monitoring, to fermentation, to drug product. There is a lot of parameter complexity around sterilization. This discussion point is another example of how this initiative is more about pharmaceutical innovation than a specific subset thereof.

Biosimilars versus Interchangeable Biologics

One of the pieces of legislation that is in debate at the moment is the Biologics Price Competition and Innovation Act (BPCIA), which seeks to provide an expedited approval framework for follow-on biologics.[*] This act will in all likelihood inform the final rules the FDA implements, and those rules will determine the business strategies of innovator companies and the extent to which generic companies use the BPCIA.

Under the BPCIA, generic biologics can be characterized as *biosimilar* to or *interchangeable* with innovator products. Both require clinical studies for approval, with interchangeability requiring a higher showing. Only those follow-on biologics designated as interchangeable can be automatically substituted by a pharmacy for the innovator's product. As a result, generic companies will have to market biosimilars to boost prescriptions and sales. Thus, when seeking approval, generic companies will weigh the cost of marketing biosimilars against the cost of the yet-to-be-determined clinical testing requirements for interchangeables. If those requirements are too onerous, the generic company may instead choose to pursue a Biologic License Application (BLA), which has the benefit of circumventing the innovator company's marketing exclusivity.

Patient safety is the biggest concern voiced by both innovator companies and patient advocacy groups, which note that little is known about biologics and any impurities or minor structural or formulation changes could have unanticipated effects for patients.

Another facet of the debate is Congress's intent: making low-cost generic biologics available to consumers. Congress probably intended something less than full clinical trials for approval of biosimilars and interchangeable biologics. But, motivated by patient safety concerns, the FDA is unlikely to implement the minimal requirements that generic companies seek. Ultimately, the FDA rules will likely provide a pathway less onerous than a BLA, but more stringent than that advocated by generic companies.

The BPCIA includes a twelve-year exclusivity period for innovator biologics to encourage continued innovation. The twelve years of exclusivity applies even if the relevant patents are found invalid or are not infringed upon during the prelaunch litigation procedures of the BPCIA.

---

[*] Adapted from DLA Piper, "Implementing the Biologics Price Competition and Innovation Act?" March 22, 2011, http://www.dlapiper.com/implementing-the-biologics-price-competition-and-innovation-act/

Given the timeframe for FDA approval of biologics, twelve years of exclusivity may provide more protection than the patent system, but that does not eliminate the need for patents. Generic companies can still file BLAs, and in some situations it may be more economical or advantageous for them to do so. Innovator companies can expect generics to choose an approval pathway based at least in part on the existence of and perceived strength of the relevant patents. The more robust the portfolio, the less likely a generic will pursue a costly BLA and at-risk launch over the BPCIA with its prelaunch litigation process.

The FDA's final rules are unlikely to end the debate surrounding the BPCIA. Whatever the rules may be, both innovator and generic companies will have to consider and pursue competitive strategies in the biologics market.

More Restrictive Regulations

Some of the changes outlined here will depend on the willingness of regulators, but there are indications that key agencies such as the Europe, Middle East, and Africa (EMEA) in Europe and the FDA in the United States are moving in these directions. PricewaterhouseCoopers (PWC) believes that by 2020, all medicines that receive approval will be approved on a real-time basis with live licenses contingent on the performance of extensive in-life testing, for specific patient subpopulations and a predetermined schedule for reviewing each set of results.[*] They also predict that the regulatory landscape will change dramatically. The public will demand independent verification of all pre- and postmarketing clinical data submitted by manufacturers. Regulatory decisions will be based on risk–benefit analyses rather than data on *comparative effectiveness* across large populations. All reviews will be accompanied by an assessment of the cost-effectiveness of new drugs, as well as safety and efficacy. And finally, increased monitoring of the treatment throughout the lifetime of a patient is more likely to occur. All of these changes will create increased complexity for the supply chain.

Increasing Use of Pervasive Monitoring

As noted earlier, healthcare policy makers and payers will increasingly use outcomes' data to determine the future application of a drug and whether

---

[*] PricewaterhouseCoopers Health Research Institute, *Pharma 2020: The Vision. Which Path Will You Take?*, 2007.

it will be covered. This means channel providers will need to build relationships with the agencies that perform the health technology assessments on which many healthcare payers will rely. Diagnostic monitoring of outcomes, combined with patient outcome counseling, will need to occur. This will be especially important in a world of bundled payments, where the fee for a medicine may be bundled with the physician services and hospital fees associated with a particular patient therapy, and the outcome is split between parties based on the patient's actual outcome. A big part of this landscape will also focus on patient compliance with a regimen. The use of remote devices to monitor patients on a real-time basis wherever they are will also allow the industry to test new medicines outside a clinical setting. The infrastructure to be able to collect information through embedded devices could be transmitted to a hub at a medical center, electronically filtered, and doses adjusted via automated systems. Driving increased compliance will not only determine whether payment will occur, it can also drive sales. Patient compliance has been a major challenge in the past. This is covered in greater detail in this chapter.

Changing Roles of Primary and Secondary Care

As noted earlier, changes in the way healthcare is delivered will require a better model than the one used today. The primary-care sector is becoming much more regimented, as general practitioners (GPs) perform more minor surgical procedures, and payers increasingly dictate the treatment protocols that must be followed.* This, of course, also includes the drugs that can be taken. The secondary-care sector is contracting, and is moving more toward secondary care at home. More self-medication is also occurring, as more prescriptions are sold in over-the-counter (OTC) formats. The definitions of primary and secondary care are blurring, and some forms of primary care are being transferred to the patient. This will further redefine distribution models. As noted in a recent report, a better understanding of the taxonomy of disease, together with better diagnostic tools and monitoring devices, will provide the means with which to bring healthcare delivery even closer to the patient. In the future, patients will be able to use web-based receiving algorithms to establish whether they have a condition that will sort itself out without recourse

* PricewaterhouseCoopers Health Research Institute, *Pharma 2020: The Vision. Which Path Will You Take?*, 2007.

to drugs. But as treatment protocols replace individual prescribing decisions, and technology improves the ability to diagnose conditions, the decision-making authority is gradually moving from doctors to healthcare policy makers and payers. What this means is that payers typically focus on risk and cost-effectiveness, whereas doctors put safety and efficacy before cost.

To summarize, these changes will mean that patient outcomes must become the focal point of any conversation involving the life sciences supply chain. If they are not, supply chain participants won't be able to leap over the infrastructural challenges that have plagued them for the last twenty to thirty years. The discussion around fee for service will increasingly move toward a need for network integration among players in the chain. Companies that do not learn to collaborate and build solutions that rely on payment for outcomes will, quite simply, disappear. Outdated financial systems and strategic planning that relies on transaction optimization, formulary negotiations, and marginal pricing will do nothing to impact whether the drug will be paid for or not in the channel. And without payment by the end customer, every entity in the chain will dry up, including physician services and hospitals themselves.

Opportunities

Despite the severity of these threats, there are hidden opportunities to be discovered here for innovators who can look beyond the current doom and gloom. Companies can initiate programs to explore value-added services, in the form of outsourced reimbursement services to providers. This can be enabled through the strong relationships that exist between key channel partners in identifying how best to deal with the complexities of this situation. Medicare Part D will result in a proliferation of different insurance providers that is likely to overwhelm and confuse the average consumer, especially the aging senior population. A one-stop-shop approach may be a potential opportunity for exploration by participants as a new business model that adds value in emerging market channels.

First, global market channel development and reimbursement models aligned with these markets will need to be developed. It seems likely that the current dominance of fee-for-service (FFS) distributing will continue in the short term in the United States, but will more than likely move toward a patient-centric value delivery model in the future. It is also increasingly clear that global markets are very much aligned with patient-centric models, and have even fewer degrees of freedom when it comes to reimbursement options. There is no doubt that the FFS distribution in the United States has certainly proven itself to have a number of advantages relative to the buy-and-hold model. Drug price increases have been restrained for a variety of reasons in the new environment, making buy-and-hold distributing less profitable. FFS distributing is more transparent because it is easier to explain to manufacturers what they are paying wholesalers for, even though there is significant disgruntlement among small and medium-sized manufacturers that are typically charged higher per-distribution service (DSP) rates. However, service providers will need to develop methods for reimbursement that share risk and rewards of the new healthcare landscape on a global scale, and develop innovative approaches to managing patient compliance, customized therapies, and pay-for-performance challenges aligned with the specific regulatory landscape for each regional growth market globally.

Second, *personalized medicine, pervasive monitoring, and patient services* hold the promise of market expansion for participants in the chain. Increased application of *patient compliance* technologies will be important here. Large wholesalers may realize some advantages relative to their smaller rivals in mail-order and Internet-based dispensing of prescription drugs. Small, unaffiliated websites and mail-order companies do not have the resources to invest in multistate licensing qualifications, whereas wholesalers do. Currently, states protect their citizens from unscrupulous Internet healthcare entities through licensing requirements for pharmacists, doctors, and wholesalers. In several other industries, state licensing laws have been struck down as being unconstitutional barriers to interstate commerce, and a similar fate could occur for pharmaceutical drugs if it becomes clear that state authorities are engaging in economic protectionism of in-state healthcare businesses.

Third, the need for ascertaining *pedigree and serialization* can provide greater visibility into the channel, meet regulatory requirements, and provide additional value-added capability in the supply chain. It seems likely that wholesalers are going to be expected to do more in the future as the regulatory challenges of compliance become more daunting. The pharmaceutical supply chain requires sophisticated wholesaling to combat the challenges posed by counterfeiting. One of the most significant services a FFS wholesaler can offer a manufacturer is licensed, environmentally controlled, Product Development and Management Association (PDMA)-compliant, secure facilities. Tracking technology is rapidly evolving from a paper-based system to more high-tech methods, particularly serialization. It seems likely that the wholesaler, or wholesalers, who are first to adopt sophisticated tracking technology will realize cost advantages relative to paper-based methods for establishing pedigree and that FDA regulations will accommodate and encourage high-tech (electronic) track and trace methods of establishing pedigree.

Fourth, the value of *specialized distribution* will become more critical, as the emergence of biologics, cold chain, and global distribution becomes more pervasive. In one possible scenario, direct sales between large manufacturers and retailers could become the norm, relegating wholesalers to servicing the currently less-profitable business of small manufacturers. A more proactive approach would be for these entities to begin to collaborate to create new market channels that bring together wholesalers, physicians, and pharmacists, enabled by electronic integration, with a focus on delivering value to the patient. Compounded by improvements in track and trace technology, transparency and linkage to patient compliance, replenishment, and inventory positioning in the global supply chain could provide a radical advantage over less-nimble competitors.

OVERVIEW OF THE BOOK

This book explores the fundamental thesis that patient-focused network integration is the only way for organizational evolution to occur in the life sciences.

Patient-centric network integration is a much more difficult approach, and requires seeing beyond the immediate tier above or below in the supply chain. Pulling together enterprises that seek to align objectives across the extended supply chain to drive operational improvement, innovation, joint outcomes, and aligned performance metrics is a core thesis that motivates this book.

Contents

As noted earlier, the chapters presented in this book are derived from hundreds of interviews with industry executives at manufacturers, group purchasing organizations (GPOs), physicians, hospitals, and wholesalers. The primary thesis we explore throughout is that a focused approach on network evolution is fundamental to change. Current models of business development will result in collapse, and doing nothing is an option that many executives seem to be stuck in. Doing nothing in this case is a *choice* that will indeed result in collapse of the system.

In an effort to promote change, I have developed seven chapters based on intensive research conducted over the last eight years. Each chapter can be viewed as an independent essay, in that it deals with a specific dimension of the healthcare value chain. However, together they provide an integrated discussion of how to begin the task of creating an integrated value chain network for healthcare. We begin with the patient, and then work our way back down the value chain, all the way to the drug development and clinical trials stage of the value chain. The common thread throughout the chapters emphasizes collaboration, strategic alignment, and a focus on delivering value to the end patient.

Chapter 2 summarizes the major trends that stretch across the three major players in the healthcare supply chain: providers, payers, and producers. Several core elements of collaboration from other industries are emphasized that are fundamental to driving integration. These elements are compared across the three elements of the value chain and a set of notable observations emerge. The elements of supply chain collaboration, in particular with other parties such as the regulatory agencies, payers, and providers, are described as being necessary for success in the years ahead, as industries are faced with the maze of pervasive monitoring and pay for performance. The need for an integrated approach is used as a basis for creating a network-based approach to solving the challenges for healthcare that lie ahead, and future predictions based on recent events are developed. A maturity model is developed that provides key milestones for delivery against this vision, and the stages of change management that must occur.

Chapter 3 explores the challenge to providers, based on multiple interviews and presentations from the most recent Integrated Distribution Network (IDN) Provider Summit in September 2012. This chapter explores the impact of the Healthcare Reform Act on hospitals, most notably Accountable Care Organizations, pay for performance, personalized medicine, and the most challenging element, bundled payments. We also identify the trends and elements ahead including the fact that primary healthcare is moving out of the physician's office into the public space, and the impact on delivery to patients and the fragmented channels that will evolve.

In Chapter 4, we review some of the findings presented in a study of how hospital providers and others in the healthcare supply chain manage supply chain data. Effective performance analytics of supply chains are absolutely essential if hospitals are to fulfill their clinical mission while managing risk and reducing cost. Yet as this analysis shows, performance analytics are one of the weakest elements in the healthcare value chain today. Without a strong analytics program, the parties in the value chain cannot exchange information. Detailed and accurate data are the foundation for controlling costs and driving effective healthcare delivery, yet this is clearly not the case, as shown in this chapter. One of the most fundamental components of a capable healthcare supply chain is the ability to carry out a category analysis using consolidated spend data at the hospital, as well as at the buyer level. This requires aggregating 100% of the data into a single consolidated view of the hospital to enable a precise analysis of how much is spent with each supplier across the health system. In this chapter, we provide results of a survey of the landscape of different providers of spend management in the healthcare industry. This included GPOs, enterprise resource planning (ERP) system providers, specialized software providers, and distributors. We assessed the accuracy and information flows for five major categories of spend management within these organizations, including the extent of data cleansing, spend analytics capabilities, contract management capabilities, technology enablement, and customer service and responsiveness. Of these, data cleansing was identified as the most challenging component that is a major barrier to healthcare value chain integration. Unfortunately, *data cleansing is also the component that was typically overlooked by the majority of the organizations reviewed in this analysis.* While each of these organizations provides a different and unique set of capabilities in the area of contract management, technology, analytics, and support, only two of the providers truly have demonstrated capabilities in capturing, cleansing, coding, and uploading 100% of the spend data for hospitals and integrated delivery networks (IDNs). Further, many of the organizations perform data cleansing only as a requirement for entering the data into their proprietary databases, without providing the cleansed dataset to the client. Without capturing and providing visibility of 100% of the spend (including not just electronic data interchange [EDI] data, but non-EDI spending, paper contracts, off-system spending, etc.), the true benefits of a strategic sourcing exercise cannot be achieved, and the result is a self-defeating exercise in futility. Only two providers of specific software targeted at data cleansing were identified in the study. This was made more complicated by the fact that up to 20% of manufacturer data that is used as input into healthcare data analysis is "dirty" or incorrect.

In Chapter 5 we report the results of a research project I completed with TraceLink, a provider of collaborative electronic technologies for the biopharmaceutical industry. I begin by discussing the current dearth of collaboration that exists, as well as the major gaps in information required to make collaborative decisions. Next, the chapter explores the important topic of aligned performance metrics in the supply chain, and the path forward for collaboration to occur. It concludes with some of the major impacts that these technologies will have in terms of the original set of challenges identified in Chapter 1.

In Chapter 6, the lagging performance of the clinical trials supply chain is explored based on results of surveys with several major biopharmaceutical companies, as well as results I presented at several biopharmaceutical conferences. The solutions to close these gaps in terms of the people, processes, and technologies for doing so are explored, and case examples from several interviews are used to illustrate how they can be implemented. We provide some guidelines for governance and management of the clinical trials supply chain.

SUMMARY

The roles of the many parties in the life science value chain continue to change and evolve. These are being changed all the more by continuous shifts in customer requirements, where the focus is on the patient as the ultimate customer, not the next party in the chain. As shown in Figure 1.4, there will be a major shift as defined by three common principles, which are emphasized in all sections of the book.

Customer Intimacy

Customers will value increased service beyond the therapeutic effect (e.g., customized packaging, customized delivery, easier payment, increased information).

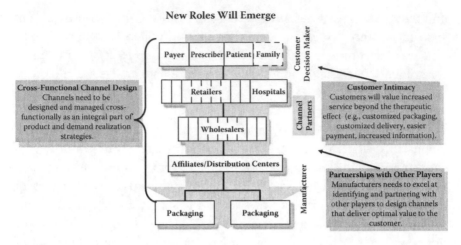

FIGURE 1.4
Redefining life science channels.

Partnerships with Other Players

Manufacturers developing and commercializing new medicines need to excel at identifying and partnering with other players to design channels that deliver optimal value to the customer.

Cross-Functional Channel Design

Channels need to be designed and managed across functions as an integral part of product and demand realization strategies.

All of the parties in the value chain, including physicians, wholesalers, retailers, manufacturers, contract manufacturers, suppliers, and clinical research organizations, need to get on board, and begin espousing these principles in their strategic plans. This book hopefully lays out a blueprint for them to get started.

2

An Evolutionary View of Healthcare Network Integration

The chapters in this book represent a series of in-depth assessments of the current state of multiple parties in the healthcare value chain, beginning with providers (hospital and physician offices), and discussing the role of payers (private healthcare insurance and Medicare/Medicaid) as well as producers (biopharmaceutical companies, contract manufacturing organizations, and contract research organizations). In order to truly make any kind of progress discussed in Chapter 1, executives will need to begin thinking differently about how they operate in the value chain. For too long, organizations have been managing based on transactional boundaries, using simple deterministic ways of thinking. This challenge is embodied in Figure 2.1.

The network of providers in healthcare is more akin to the dynamics associated with complex systems. Complex systems theory grapples with how organizations adapt in the face of dynamic change and evolve over time, with those organizations best able to adapt ultimately surviving.[*] A further branch of thinking suggests that firms that are able to survive essentially do so through coevolving with those entities around them. This line of thought, sometimes called the *resource-based view*, suggests that the changing relationship between a firm's activities and entities in its competitive environment creates whatever distinct capabilities it draws on for sustained competitive advantage.[†] In simpler terms, the organizational processes that occur with other entities in the value chain together provide the *emergent* strategies that shape how the organization survives.

---

[*] H. Aldrich, 1979. *Organizations and Environments* (Englewood Cliffs, NJ: Prentice Hall, 1979).

[†] Many scholars have contributed to this line of thought. A good summary of these references is provided by Bill McKelvey, "Avoiding Complexity Catastrophe in Coevolutionary Pockets: Strategies for Rugged Landscapes," *Organization Science* 10, no. 3 (1999): 294–231.

Key Issues Facing the Industry	R&D	Clinical	Manufacturing & CMOs	Wholesalers & 3PL Providers	Payers Hospitals Physicians	Customer Patient
• Growing adoption of price restrictions by regulators and governments • Declining R&D productivity • Increasing emphasis on personalized medicine and pay for performance • Fragmentation of global mass markets • Emergence of biotech and biological treatments as predominant growth markets • Biosimilars and interchangeable biologics • More restrictive clinical evidence • Increased use of pervasive monitoring • Changing role of primary and secondary care			How do the players in the value chain work together through relational contracting to create innovative solutions to these massive challenges?			

FIGURE 2.1
Supply network/customer channel.

Darwinian selectionist theory proposes that living things evolve as their parts (organs, biomolecules, or genes) mutate. Along these lines, organization theorists would suggest that organizations adapt as each of the supply chain competencies (representing microagents—the individual activities that make up the entire organization) influence selective advantage for the firm as a whole.[*] Again, translating this into operational thinking, organizations that drive collaborative behavior with their key supply chain partners in their daily routines, contracting approaches, and relationships, coevolve to a higher level of performance that allows all entities in the chain to not only survive, but adapt to the rapidly changing environment around it. More importantly, "in co-evolutionary processes, the fitness of one organism or species depends on the characteristics of the other organisms or species with which it interacts, while all simultaneously adapt and change."[†] This evolution occurs even in an environment that is characterized by rapid change, regulatory pressure, new technology,

---

[*] S. A. Kauffman, *The Origins of Order: Self-Organization and Selection in Evolution* (New York: Oxford University Press, 1993).
[†] Kauffman, *The Origins of Order*, 33.

and other major challenges. As Kauffman notes, "A critical difference between evolution on a fixed landscape and coevolution is that the former can be roughly characterized as if it were an adapt search on a 'potential surface' or 'fitness surface,' whose peaks are the positions sought. In coevolution, there may typically be no such potential surface, and the process is far more complex."*

The implication here is that organizations in the value chain must begin to think of not only their local environments, but extend their strategies to consider all of the participants in the value chain. This is shown in Figure 2.2. In particular, focus should be directed at the patient, who is the ultimate customer in the system, and whose health is ultimately the real objective sought by all parties in the chain. The problem, of course, is that patient disease is also a moving target, and as we know more about the origins of disease, we are coming to understand that a single molecular entity often does not address all of the needs of all patients we are trying to serve. This is a true innovation, as entities in the value chain begin to drive solutions that link analytics, performance outcomes, and ultimately, patient value. While this approach is intuitively sound, sorting out the elements of how to achieve it has been elusive for many.

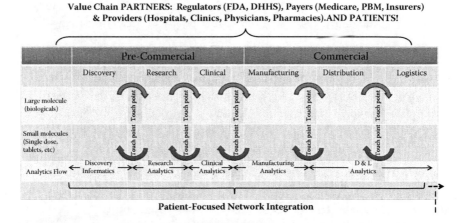

FIGURE 2.2
Biopharmaceutical industry innovation.

---

* Kauffman, *The Origins of Order*, 33.

All organizations evolve based on the application of rules or based on following a certain set of performance metrics that indicate progress toward those rules. The problem, or course, is that adherence to these rules may lead to evolution, but not all evolutions lead to successful adaptations to the environment.* Many organizations may be following the wrong set of rules, or even if their intent is to improve, they are using the wrong set of performance metrics to indicate whether adequate progress is being made toward the right evolutionary outcome.

A recent set of discussions with biopharmaceutical and pharmaceutical companies revealed the challenges they are facing with respect to planning for performance given the uncertainty of the current healthcare environment. One executive noted the following:

> What happens is, we have thresholds for our KPIs (key performance indicators), and those thresholds are supposed to tell us how well we are performing. When we operate and take measurements, however, we don't do it until after the fact. We are concerned that a product is being manufactured, released, and sent into the distribution chain. But what we don't see are the current inventory levels, the firefighting, the expediting that occurs, which is really indicative of how well we are managing our value chain. Every quarter our managers go into the systems, collect the data, calculate KPIs, and see how they are performing, and present them in a quarterly business review meeting. And only then do we discover how poorly we are performing!

A key entity that is shaping the environment is the regulatory agencies, as well as the payers. Entities (or should we say organisms) include the Food and Drug Administration (FDA), health insurance payers, the Department of Homeland Security, and other key entities in the United States and a host of government agencies throughout the world. These entities need to be drawn into the value chain network and consulted more often.

These elements represent the foundation of what we hope to achieve in this book. I believe that a formal structure for building network integration capabilities is required for every organization in the value chain. The overall maturity structure shown in Figure 2.3 identifies some of the key characteristics of change management that I have found to be critical stepping stones for integration of any industrial supply chain. I believe these elements are also critical for maturing the healthcare value

---

* Benoit Morel and Rangaraj Ramanujam, "Through the Looking Glass of Complexity: The Dynamics of Organizations as Adaptive and Evolving Systems," *Organization Science* 10, no. 3 (1999): 278–293.

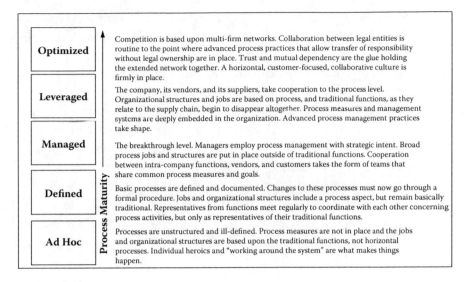

Optimized	Competition is based upon multi-firm networks. Collaboration between legal entities is routine to the point where advanced process practices that allow transfer of responsibility without legal ownership are in place. Trust and mutual dependency are the glue holding the extended network together. A horizontal, customer-focused, collaborative culture is firmly in place.
Leveraged	The company, its vendors, and its suppliers, take cooperation to the process level. Organizational structures and jobs are based on process, and traditional functions, as they relate to the supply chain, begin to disappear altogether. Process measures and management systems are deeply embedded in the organization. Advanced process management practices take shape.
Managed	The breakthrough level. Managers employ process management with strategic intent. Broad process jobs and structures are put in place outside of traditional functions. Cooperation between intra-company functions, vendors, and customers takes the form of teams that share common process measures and goals.
Defined	Basic processes are defined and documented. Changes to these processes must now go through a formal procedure. Jobs and organizational structures include a process aspect, but remain basically traditional. Representatives from functions meet regularly to coordinate with each other concerning process activities, but only as representatives of their traditional functions.
Ad Hoc	Processes are unstructured and ill-defined. Process measures are not in place and the jobs and organizational structures are based upon the traditional functions, not horizontal processes. Individual heroics and "working around the system" are what makes things happen.

FIGURE 2.3
Supply chain process maturity.

chain. In this chapter, we adapt this framework to tie together the core changes that must occur in supply chain governance, planning, metrics, risk management, transition, and talent development. We then elaborate on and allude to these elements throughout the remainder of the book.

- **Governance:** This element involves the roles, responsibilities, and decision-making process used to govern all major strategic and tactical decisions across the value chain network.
- **Network culture:** This element is the value attached to collaborative decision making that exists in an organization, and involves the extent to which individuals are willing to "play fair" with others in the network, share information, and create joint decisions that will mutually share risks and rewards across the network.
- **Management system performance analytics:** This element involves the quality and accuracy of data upon which decisions are made, and the level of capability to derive analytical models is based on sound data that provide scenario analysis, risk analysis, total cost analysis, and improved efficiency and performance across the network. In a best-case scenario, metrics should be aligned with end-patient needs.
- **Risk management:** This element is the ability to quantify and identify risks and to mitigate and reduce risk exposure in the value network.

The major types of supply chain disruptions and operational issues related to risk include patient safety, drug shortages, financial risk, operational risk, and litigation risk.

- **Technology management:** This element is the ability to develop clinical medicines that align with other stakeholder needs in the network and that align patient outcome value with cost. Targeted therapies are an example of technology that holds the promise to develop drugs with effectiveness that is comparable relative to other medicines on the market.
- **Talent development:** This element is the development of a pipeline of individuals who are capable of bringing innovative solutions to the value chain, and who are able to lead others in improving the value to all members in the network.

CORE ELEMENTS FOR NETWORK INTEGRATION

Although physicians are at the core of hospitals and healthcare, there are many reasons why the power is being drained from physicians in the system. These are described more in the book. This power is increasingly moving to payers (Medicare, government regulatory bureaucrats, and insurance companies). Producers (commercial entities that develop and manufacture drugs) are also being held to tighter regulation, and are assuming in many cases that payers will have no other choice but to pay the high cost of new biologics. This is also not an assumption that necessarily holds true in an era of healthcare reform. As this occurs, it is therefore important to consider how the core theme of collaboration and network integration will play a critical role in the attainment of patient value and enterprise profitability— two elements that are not at odds with one another. A description of the elements of change in a maturity model is offered next.

WHAT IS A MATURITY MODEL?

Organizations that go about any improvement initiative go through a series of changes that determine the speed and effectiveness of change. Just like a human begins to sit up, crawl, then walk, and then run, organizational maturity comes in five stages, ultimately reaching an end goal of having a completely extended organization with full integration of activities among companies, their customers, and their trading partners. Each successive step includes more functions and more firms within a given supply chain. A brief description of a generic five-stage maturity model that reflects increasing supply chain process maturity is shown in Figure 2.3, and a contextual interpretation of what this means for healthcare providers (hospitals and insurance companies) is shown in Figure 2.4. (Note that Figure 2.4 has collapsed Stages 4 and 5 into a single category for simplification.)

What an enterprise does at each step and how it does it are equally important. For example, if it performs regular sales forecasts based on historical data and mathematical models, it is just as important that the company employs this data in a collaborative fashion, providing it to key groups both inside and outside the company. The *what* and the *how* are both relevant here.

The five stages of maturity shown in Figures 2.3 and 2.4 describe the progression of activities toward effective healthcare supply chain integration. These are the five stages:

- **Ad Hoc:** The supply chain and the network practices are unstructured and ill defined. Process measures are not in place, and the jobs and organizational structures are based upon the traditional functions, not horizontal supply chain processes. Individual heroics and "working around the system" are what make things happen.
- **Defined:** The basic network processes are defined and documented. The order commitment, procurement, and other processes, for example, are available in flow charts, and changes to these processes must now go through a formal procedure. Jobs and organizational structures include a network culture aspect, but remain basically traditional. Representatives from different functions (physicians, payers, planners) meet regularly to coordinate with each other, but only as representatives of their traditional functions. Similarly, functional representatives meet to coordinate schedules with vendors and customers.
- **Managed:** This is the breakthrough level. Managers employ supply chain management (SCM) with strategic intent and results. Broad network jobs and structures are put in place outside of traditional functions. One common indicator is the appearance of the title

Network Partners = CMOs, Suppliers, Co-Mfg. Partners, Wholesalers, Retailers, Hospitals, Physicians, Payers, & Patients!

Initiatives	Ad Hoc No Process	Defined Reactive	Managed/Standard	Leveraged Advanced
Governance	Physician acts independently based on "cowboy" mentality	Internal consultation with other physicians	Regular reviews of options with patients and payers Preventive care policies. Regular 3rd party engagement	Aligned patient council with key network partners and reporting structure are major decision points
Network Culture	Silo physician culture Single decisions with little patient or 3rd–party review	Process defined & documented. Some compliance to payer requirements	Regular patient discussions with payers and providers	Network partners (Suppliers, payers, etc.) engaged in strategic patient reviews
Management Systems & Analytics	Independent patient records	Patient analytics in an electric health record	Physician performance tied to patient outcomes as measured by EHR. Should-cost and total–cost models used to drive payer negotiations and policies	EHR linked to aligned metrics, milestones and contract mgmt with networked partners by segment. Social media/alternative technologies used to drive transparency
Patient Disease (Risk) Management	Firefighting and mitigation based on appearance of symptoms	Diagnosis based on patient history and monitoring	Biomarkers and genetic analysis provides early warning of potential diseases and preventive medical treatment	Lifelong patient monitoring by third parties with specialized delivery and monitoring through social media
Administering and Deployment of Technologies/Therapies	Hard handover from R&D to physician	Transition team documents learning and feedback	Multiprovider/payer/physician team approach to evaluate holistically	Early integration of key network partners into therapeutic and technology decisions
Talent Development	Little technology knowledge	Physicians team skills introduced into medical schools, along with technological savvy	Team building and technology integration linked with physician professional career path and therapeutic monitoring of patients	Physician and patients are actively engaged and communicating with biopharma companies
	Current	2–5 years	8–12 years	

FIGURE 2.4

Patient-focused network integration for providers (hospitals, physician offices).

supply chain manager in the organization. Cooperation among intracompany functions, suppliers, and customers takes the form of teams that share common performance measures and goals that reach horizontally across the supply chain.

- **Leveraged:** The company, its vendors, and suppliers take cooperation to the process level. Organizational structures and jobs are based on SCM procedures, and traditional functions, as they relate to the supply chain, begin to disappear altogether. Network measures and management systems are deeply embedded in the organization. Advanced networkwide practices take shape.

- **Optimized:** Competition is based on multifirm supply chains. Collaboration between legal entities is routine to the point where advanced network practices that allow transfer of responsibility without legal ownership are in place. Trust and mutual dependency are the glue holding the extended supply chain together. A horizontal, customer-focused, collaborative culture is firmly in place.

For each of the dimensions of network maturity, we provide a set of implications for providers (hospitals) and payers (insurance companies and Medicare) in this chapter. The themes of value chain collaboration, network analytics, governance, and talent management are discussed in some detail as they relate to healthcare providers here. As shown in Figures 2.5 and 2.6, the maturity model applies equally to other parties in the value chain, but may involve a somewhat different context. For payers (Figure 2.5), the emphasis is on synchronized planning and analytics. For producers (manufacturers and contract manufacturing organizations [CMOs]), Figure 2.6 shows many of the multiple product development, clinical trials, manufacturing process planning, and quality handoffs that require alignment and collaboration. The specific context and explication of these network maturity frameworks is a thread that is applied in the remainder of this book. In Chapter 3, we further elaborate on the principles of the maturity model as they apply to healthcare providers. In Chapter 4, we utilize a maturity model to benchmark spend analytics solutions in healthcare providers. In Chapter 5, on supply chain planning, we also provide a global maturity model for electronic collaboration for producers (manufacturers, suppliers and CMOs). In Chapter 6, we provide a more structured and detailed maturity model for clinical research organizations conducting clinical trials.

Network Partners = CMOs, Suppliers, Co-Mfg. Partners, Wholesalers, Retailers, Hospitals, Physicians, Payers, & Patients!

Initiatives	Ad Hoc No Process	Defined Reactive	Managed/Standard	Leveraged Advanced
Governance	No formal approach for comparative effectiveness of drugs established	Multi-functional teams with defined roles & responsibilities	Regular reviews of comparative effectiveness with other providers	Aligned industry council with key network partners and reporting structure quarterly
Planning Culture	Silo culture silo'd decisions with little x-functional review/input	Process defined & documented Some compliance to process	Strategy reviews & debate. Regular 3rd party intelligence reviews	Network partners (Suppliers, distributors, etc.) engaged in strategic planning reviews
Planning & Performance Metrics	Sales, finance, operations plans diverge Excel spreadsheets	Pilot analytics system at product family level	Synchronized planning and aligned performance metrics and analytics across multiple medicine areas	Globally aligned metrics, milestones and integration with clinical trials providers focusing on biomarkers and targeted costs therapies
Risk Management	Firefighting and mitigation based on "best guess"	Multi-tiered approvals based on physician advisory panels	Detailed comprehensive cost effectiveness studies utilizing on-going patient databases and effectiveness data collected through reliance on multiple primary and secondary network sources	Dynamic auto generation of risk alerts in the network based on market intelligence and risk
Technology	Hard handover from R&D to commercial	Transition team documents key handoff requirements	End-to-end network collaboration on new product requirements shared	Early integration of key network partners into New Product Introduction (NPI) decisions
Talent Development	Lack of career path and talent acquisition strategy	Network integration skills and competencies defined and assessed	Defined professional career path into network integration requiring multi-functional business team mentoring	Executives-on-loan from key partners utilized to share learning in the network
	Current	2–5 years	8–12 years	

FIGURE 2.5

Network maturity for payers (health insurers, Medicare, Medicaid).

Network Partners = CMOs, Suppliers, Co-Mfg. Partners, Wholesalers, Retailers, Hospitals, Physicians, Payers, & Patients!

Initiatives	Ad Hoc No Process	Defined Reactive	Managed Standard	Leveraged Advanced
Governance	No formal global insource/outsource strategy team; few policies or roles established	Multi-functional with defined roles & responsibilities	Regular reviews of plans Strategy reviews & debate Regular 3rd–party intelligence reviews	Aligned council with key network partners and reporting structure quarterly
Planning Culture	Silo culture silo'd decisions with little x-functional review/input	Process defined & documented Some compliance to process	Regular strategy reviews attended by all participants	Network partners (Suppliers, distributors, etc.) engaged in strategic planning reviews
Planning & Performance Metrics	Sales, finance, operations plans diverge. Excel spreadsheets	Pilot analytics system at product family level	Synchronized planning and aligned performance metrics and analytics across LOBs	Globally aligned metrics, milestones and contract mgmt with networked partners
Risk Management	Firefighting and mitigation based on "best guess"	Targeted approach to establish secondary metrics	Analytics COE relies on multiple primary and secondary network sources	Dynamic auto generation of risk alerts in the network based on social media and other mechanisms
NPI to Commercialization	Hard handover from R&D to commercial	Transition team documents key handoff requirements	Mfg/SCM/Pack Mgmt/Sales represented on NPI/Clinical team to ensure early input	Early integration of key network partners into NPI decisions
Talent Development	Lack of career path and talent acquisition strategy	Network integration skills and competencies defined and assessed	Defined professional career path into network integration requiring multi-functional business team mentoring	Executives-on-loan from key partners utilized to share learning in the network

FIGURE 2.6
Network maturity for producers (CMOs and manufacturers).

Next, we focus on the application of the healthcare maturity model to healthcare providers.

GOVERNANCE: HEALTHCARE

In the context of healthcare providers, governance requires a fundamental shift in the culture and thinking of physicians. As Gawande[*] notes, "the core structure of medicine emerged in an era when doctors could hold all the key information patients needed in their heads and manage everything required themselves. ... We were craftsmen. ... The nature of the knowledge lent itself to prizing autonomy, independence, and self-sufficiency among our highest values, and to designing medicine accordingly." The environment we find ourselves in today is diametrically opposite. Today, physicians operate as part of a team, as there are so many diverse technologies, specialties, and protocols associated with a disease that a team of experts is required to address the issue. The other important difference is that cost is now an important part of the equation going into the decision, and not just an outcome of a physician's decision. As such, the accounting team and the payer are part of this team because they provide input on what is within a reasonable budget given the expected value of the patient outcome. Like it or not, cost is now an imperative in the environment in which we find ourselves. As such, physicians need to be able to act more like a team, and the best outcome is certainly not going to be at the highest cost in every situation.

The closest approximation to this concept is that of value engineering, where a design team evaluates different materials, technologies, and production methods that produce the optimal product performance characteristics. Options may include changing the specifications, utilizing an alternative material, reducing the number of parts, and so on. In the same manner, a patient outcome is a function of different potential therapies, medicines, treatment plans, or ideally, preventive behaviors undertaken before symptoms of the problem become evident. Too often today there is no consistent sense in the way that physicians interact with one another and evaluate alternatives to provide a system of care for people. In the metaphor provided by Gawande, physicians are trained, hired, and paid to be cowboys, but it is really pit crews

---

[*] Gawande, A. Healthcare Needs a New Kind of Hero. *Harvard Business Review,* 88, no. 4 (2010): 60–61.

that people need. Pit crews work as a team to provide an efficient, reliable outcome involving quick diagnosis, application of methods, and aligned decision making that meet the need, at minimal expense.

As such, governance of patient medical decisions should include not just a team of aligned "tag-team" physicians, as well as payers and biopharmaceutical/medical device manufacturers, but include the patient as well. The patient must be provided with full disclosure on outcomes, and also be made aware of the fact that there is a cost factor that needs to be considered, and that unbridled spending is not an option unless there is demonstrable evidence that the diagnosis and prescription are aligned and that optimal efficacy is planned. In this sense, there is a need for a patient-focused governance council, whereby the patient is advised by a multiparticipant council that includes representation or interface with the provider of the medication, the payer, the hospital, and the patient.

Clearly, this is not an activity that occurs for every patient encounter. In this sense, we are promoting an activity that is utilized for major healthcare decisions. The provider that comes closest to this model is the Mayo Clinic, which incidentally, has as its primary statement "The needs of the patient come first," but which is driven by its mission statement: "To inspire hope and contribute to health and well-being by providing the best care to every patient through integrated clinical practice, education and research."* At the Mayo, all physicians associated with a disease are consulted to provide a 360-degree view with multiple inputs, to provide a holistic set of insights resulting in a more objective diagnosis. What we are proposing in our network model (Figure 2.4) is an extension of this approach that includes suppliers and payers in this dialogue, to provide a networked view of patient care.

NETWORK CULTURE

This type of networked approach is clearly a radical shift from what we have seen in the past. How can this approach be enabled? Electronic health records are certainly a start, and provide a common view and sheet of music that all parties can view (with patient permission), and a common set of patient histories. But that isn't enough. Such records, as we have seen, will need to be augmented with monitoring history for medications

---

* Mayo Clinic, "Mayo Clinic Mission and Values," Mayo Clinic, http://www.mayoclinic.org/about/ missionvalues.html, 2001–2012.

and treatments, to show compliance against the regimen, and incentives to do so. One of the ways to drive this culture is through the application of systematic approaches to alignment. Physicians will need to become much more of team players and be willing to admit that they might be wrong. As Atul Gawande pointed out to a group of graduating Harvard medical students, the values required include "humility, an understanding that no matter who you are, how experienced or smart, you will fail. They include discipline, the belief that standardization, doing certain things the same way every time, can reduce your failures. And they include teamwork, the recognition that others can save you from failure, no matter who they are in the hierarchy. ... Resistance also surfaces because medicine is not structured for group work. Even just asking clinicians to make time to sit together and agree on plans for complex patients feels like an imposition."[*]

The current state of provider–payer integration is in fact moving in the opposite direction in some cases. For example, in Pittsburgh, Pennsylvania, the largest healthcare integrated distribution network is the University of Pittsburgh Medical Center (UPMC), which has its own insurance services (UPMC Health Plan). The second-largest provider in the state is the Western Pennsylvania Allegheny Hospital System (WPAHS). In June 2011, the largest insurer in the state of Pennsylvania, Highmark Blue Cross Blue Shield of Pennsylvania and WPAHS announced their intention to pursue an affiliation aimed at maintaining the health system as a high-quality choice for healthcare services to millions of Western Pennsylvanians. Under these terms, Highmark will refuse to pay for patient care at UPMC, which will also refuse to pay for treatment at WPAHS. In effect, patients have to choose which health plan they want, and local community enterprises such as Westinghouse are allowing their employees to pick which health plan they want to use. In effect, Highmark is the lower-cost provider, and as such, may offer a lower set of premiums to individuals. This may one day lead to insurance exchanges, whereby individuals who are younger and healthier may pick a lower-cost payer, whereas others who are older and have a greater diversity of needs may want to pay more for more coverage.

This culture change may also include the use of checklists and consultative meetings with suppliers and payers, to go through the potential options. Checklists are one of the most basic tools of quality and productivity in aviation, engineering, and construction—so why not medicine? Similarly,

---

[*] Atul Gawande, 2011. "Cowboys and Pit Crews," Commencement address, Harvard Medical School, May 2011.

team-based network outcomes involving teams of engineers, suppliers, and customers focused on technical problems are also par for the course in many industries—so why not healthcare? This is a radical new approach to the challenges being posed by bundled payments and pay for performance, and requires a fundamental shift in physicians' attitudes. No longer just responsible for a single diagnosis based on a five-minute patient visit, this will mean greater understanding of analytics and a more consultative approach with patients and suppliers. But how can this be achieved given the already pressing time constraints in the system?

The message for biopharma companies is that they need to better understand the network of healthcare providers that is emerging in the new world. These parties are segmented as shown in Figure 2.7, which was developed by Harry Winston* of IBM's Healthcare and Life Sciences team. He points out that the three primary destinations of care for baby boomers coming into old age will be as follows:

- **Acute care:** Specialty clinics, community hospitals, and intensive care units (ICUs)
- **Residential care:** Assisted living and skilled nursing facilities

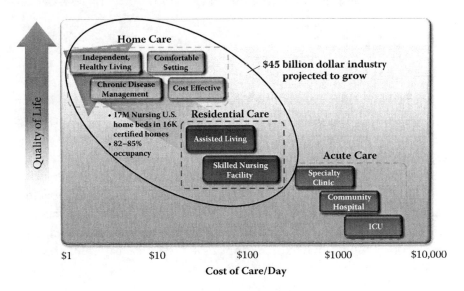

FIGURE 2.7
Changing destinations of care.

* Harry Winston, 2011. Presentation to North Carolina Executive Programs, Raleigh: NC. December 16, 2011.

- **Home care:** Independent healthy patients living at home in a comfortable setting, who have a chronic disease that needs be managed in a cost-effective manner

For each of these segments, a different approach to delivering and administering therapies needs to be considered and aligned with product development, clinical trials, and research and development (R&D) strategies. There are also significant differences in the cost of care per day in each of these settings, as well as a differentiated level of quality of life for patients in these environments. The optimal condition for patient care is, of course, high quality of life and lowest cost per day, but distribution and feedback technologies for each of these modes needs to be given some thought. There is no one-size-fits-all delivery or cost model, and biopharma companies need to give some thought as to how they will set up business systems, monitoring mechanisms, and patient care systems with these different players in the ecosystem. A network culture recognizes that regular communication, transparency, and patient feedback mechanisms is fundamental to creating successful patient outcomes. Monitoring mechanisms that provide feedback into the biopharma systems for dosing, results, responses, and new hypotheses for the next generation of therapies is critical.

PERFORMANCE ANALYTICS

One of the key differences that will enable this transition is the introduction of electronic health records (EHRs). Although viewed as a massive investment providing dubious value by many, EHRs are in fact the critical enabler that will allow this networked approach to function. By having a "single sheet of music," the entire orchestra of medical providers, biopharmaceutical companies, payers, and device manufacturers can play together in harmony. EHRs are not just static documents—I am thinking about a time when they will be linked to patient dosing, medical treatment compliance, critical signs and diet monitoring, and preventive care activities. Did you go for a run today? If so, you will include this in your calendar, which will link it to your EHR showing that you are keeping up with your schedule.

It is also important to consider the different environments in which healthcare providers and payers will be interacting with patients, which is shown in Figure 2.7. As shown, the primary emerging care models will fall into one of five categories, each of which will have a very different set of systems and feedback mechanisms into which biopharma companies will need to tap.

1. **Accountable care organizations (ACOs):** As we noted earlier, ACOs will have a regimented set of cost requirements mandated by government or insurance payers. In this context, there will be a direct line of sight between the provider and the patient, so control will be greater. Systems integration will emerge through partnerships with these institutions and have dedicated and linked systems and technologies with nurses and administrators.

2. **Patient-centered medical homes:** This format will also have a greater influence in terms of patient care, but there may still be some self-administration of services. As such, a hybrid of integration mechanisms will be required.

3. **Specialty care models:** These centers will focus on oncology or complex cardiology, and tight integration with physicians and monitoring equipment will need to occur, as these may often be specialized clinics.

4. **Episode of care:** Centers will include acute, episodic surgeries such as joint replacement, coronary artery bypass grafting (CABG), or heart attacks (acute myocardial infarction, or AMI). These surgical procedures will again require intensive technology integration with patient records technologies in operating rooms, and postsurgical monitoring after the patient leaves the care of the provider and returns home. A hybrid approach that uses intensive monitoring for inpatient and social media/handheld monitoring of outpatient care will be required.

5. **Clinical service factories:** As we noted earlier, day-to-day secondary care is moving more to service factories, such as a Walmart or walk-in clinics with nurse practitioners rather than direct physician interfaces. These clinics will need to have EHRs tied to patient integrated systems that feed back patient dosage and prescriptions, and once the patient leaves the clinic, compliance and monitoring technology. The amount of data required to monitor patients is staggering in scope, and we may not see this for several years to come.

Another key component that will drive performance and decision making is the application of *should-cost* and *total cost* models. Cost models have been applied for years in engineering and product development and were pioneered by companies such as Honda. The concept is to develop a model of what a "typical" procedure should cost, and then allow for variances both up and down in terms of discrepancies, variation in patients, and normal operating procedures. After years of interviews with physicians and payers, I have yet to see anyone consider the application of such models in healthcare. And yet the concept of *bundled payments*, by its very definition, will require capabilities that allow organizations to allocate costs and attribute them to different cost drivers, as well as identify patient outcomes. Proactive providers will develop these capabilities in negotiating rates with payers, and this ideally should be a collaborative process that is data-driven in nature, and used to drive productive discussions about policies that can drive down costs. The case at the end of Chapter 3 provides a good example of how a good cost model can drive physician engagement in a decision.

PATIENT AND DISEASE MANAGEMENT

Physicians today are more likely to act and think as independents who are confident of their own abilities and often get into heated debates with other medical professionals when it comes to diagnosis and opinions. While a certain amount of debate makes sense, the fact is that physicians aren't the only ones with a stake in the game. Increasingly, insurers are buying health-care providers, or seeking to work with them on new cooperative deals and payment models that share the risks of health coverage. A recent study by Accenture shows that by 2013, less than one-third of all physicians will own their own practices, and the majority (67%) will be employed by hospitals or agencies with strong ties to insurance companies.[*] This means that doctors' diagnoses will increasingly be biased toward an economic incentive, as their salary will be coming from an agency that has direct incentives to control costs. Doctors will be asked to reduce the number of external physician referrals, and reduce the number of expensive clinical and laboratory tests they recommend to their patients. Already, physicians such as those at hospital systems in Massachusetts have their pay tied to patient satisfaction, quality, and efficiency goals, which are a mix of their own efforts and those of the entire physician group. The quality portion includes measures such as patient blood pressure control and preventive care like mammograms. Efficiency is tied to statistics, including how often doctors refer patients to specialists outside the system and how often patients go to the emergency room.[†]

---

[*] Anna Wilde Mathews, "The Future of Healthcare," *Wall Street Journal*, December 12, 2011.
[†] Ibid.

For life science companies, this will mean thinking very differently about the healthcare ecosystem, and how organizations develop and deliver medicines to this team of stakeholders (which still includes physicians, but also payers and healthcare providers). IBM's Institute for Business Value* identifies several questions that life science companies need to consider as they develop strategic postures and transform themselves from siloed providers of pills and vials, to providers of health system enablers.

- Is your company focused on patients or people? Patients are individuals who show up as blind data in a sales report that is handled by someone else. When viewed as people, life sciences' companies may begin to think about the offerings that address a person with the condition, as well as the care team that surrounds that person.
- Is your organization focused on disease or on health? A focus on disease leads to a focus on driving a medication to treat a disease. Alternatively, a focus on health may also include thinking about prevention and wellness, as well as the early indicators that can serve as biomarkers to prevent it.
- Is your company a supplier or a partner? A supplier produces a product that is shipped to a customer, and the obligation is fulfilled. A true partner thinks about the entire set of payers and providers in the ecosystem and the ultimate requirements of the patients they serve. The focus is on outcomes and lowering overall healthcare costs.

The answers to these deep questions will determine how well biopharma will interface and grow with the maturing of healthcare providers into patient treatment and disease management.

ADMINISTERING AND DEPLOYING TECHNOLOGIES AND THERAPIES

Today's research organizations in preclinical studies are primarily engaged in understanding how to treat or manage diseases. Occasionally, a drug is discovered that can actually cure a disease, but this is exceptionally rare.

---

* IBM Institute for Business Value, *"Fade or Flourish? Rethinking the Role of Life Sciences Companies in the Healthcare Ecosystem,"* IBM Corporation, 2011.

When a target is identified, it is moved into a clinical phase where animals and humans go through clinical trials to derive empirical evidence of the drug's safety and efficacy. Nowhere in this process is there any evidence of a discussion of target costs, payer requirements, patient preferences, or ability to pay. The assumption is that if we produce it, they will come. Another consideration should include how the drug is administered, delivered, and complied with to be effective. The case of oncology provides a good example.

As cancer fast overcomes heart disease as the leading cause of death and disease in the United States, chemotherapeutics, biotechnology drugs, and other treatment options will correspondingly lead the way with increased utilization and higher treatment costs in the foreseeable future. One of the key issues here is that pharmacists will play a more pivotal role in managing not only the clinical, but also the financial aspects of patient care. As stand-alone, community-based cancer centers and physician-office-based treatment facilities proliferate and chemotherapy agents become more complex, the demand for board-certified oncology pharmacists is growing. A recent study estimated that 70% to 80% of large oncology practices employ pharmacists and pharmacy technicians.[*]

Pharmacists have proven a valuable asset for several reasons. Not only are pharmacists familiar with drug protocols and experts when it comes to dealing with drug interactions, but oncologists also frequently rely on them for recommending dosage adjustments in patients whose disease is complex. At some comprehensive cancer centers, pharmacists preside over the preparation of injectable agents by pharmacy technicians. Increasingly, the pharmacist's role is expanding beyond clinical duties. For example, in many facilities, pharmacists oversee drug purchases. Recently, a Congressional Medicare Payment Advisory Commission recommended that community-based oncology practices, in order to reduce costs and improve efficiency, hire pharmacists to buy and prepare medications and recommend drug products based on price and clinical effectiveness.[*] More and more large community-based oncology centers are installing on-site retail pharmacies where a staff pharmacist not only fills oral prescriptions, but in some cases prepares compounds and medications.

---

[*] Chris Nee, Pharm.D., M.B.A., President, PharMedQuest, *Oncology Drug Management: A White Paper on Marketplace Challenges, Opportunities and Strategies*, Atlantic Information Services, Inc., and PharMedQuest, March 2007.

The point here is that pharmacists, not just physicians, will play a pivotal role in the delivery of drugs to patients, not just for oncology, but for other drugs. Other important players in the provider community will also be more important. Biopharma companies need to give more thought to who will be in the mix and the core caregivers and advisors that form the consultative team for a patient. Understanding the requirements and obtaining input from these key constituents will be critical for success.

THE CASE OF ORPHAN DISEASES

Perhaps no other case for a new approach for targeting cost is better than the case of orphan drugs. Orphan diseases are a growing concern in many healthcare circles and have recently been identified as a major source of concern for state healthcare plans. Due to this concern, states are seeking to shift some of the burden of orphan medicines to patients, much to the patients' concern (Pollack 2012). Orphan diseases and orphan drugs (OD) are referred to in several contexts, including *rare disease, orphan medicine, rare medicine,* and so on, and are a subject of intense study in pharmacoeconomics and cost-effectiveness research (Denis et al. 2010; PhRMA Rare Diseases Report 2011; Brewer 2009). By some estimates, 8%–10% of Americans (some 20–25 million) have one of the nearly 7,000 diseases that are often deemed *rare* because alone they each affect fewer than 200,000 people (PhRMA 2011). In some cases, only a few hundred are known to have a particular rare disease. There have been more than 350 OD product approvals since the Orphan Drug Act in 1983 (as opposed to fewer than ten in the 1970s), positively impacting as many as 12 million Americans. Today, many new ODs are in the pipeline, which is positive news for patients and for their physicians. Diseases with the highest number of orphan drug designations include autoimmune deficiency syndrome (AIDS) (57), melanoma (51), cystic fibrosis (46), acute myeloid leukemia (34), ovarian cancer (34), and pancreatic cancer (33) (Braun 2010).

In 1982, the National Organization for Rare Diseases was founded. It formed two committees, leading to the passing by President Ronald Reagan, of the Orphan Drug Act in 1983 (Brewer 2009). The act provided incentives for manufacturers to develop more than 350 orphan disease drugs. Some of the benefits included a longer period of marketing exclusivity for drugs that may not recoup their development costs or that are targeted at diseases affecting fewer than 200,000 people. More than 2,313 medicines had been designated as orphan drugs by the FDA as of January 24, 2011. While this is good news for patients who suffer from these diseases, the issue has become of growing concern for healthcare providers and payers faced with the rising costs of OD drugs (Denis et al. 2009) As noted by the *New York Times* article, states are also seeking to shift the cost burden of these drugs back onto patients, which also risks limiting patient access, especially in cases when clear cost-effectiveness studies are lacking.

Manufacturers were quick to respond to the incentives provided for them in the Orphan Drug Act. As the flow of blockbusters shrunk to a trickle, the industry has begun to restructure itself to make a profit on patient populations under 200,000. Much of this has occurred through partnerships with academic institutions (Brewer 2006; 2009). While the FDA has shifted toward academic orphan drug research, some suggest that restructuring of the pharmaceutical industry and health systems is needed to promote ongoing orphan drug research (Brewer 2009).

Research by Handfield and Feldstein (in progress) suggests that an entirely new approach is needed to make more cost-effective yet fair decisions when it comes to reimbursement of orphan disease drugs. The health system in the United Kingdom, for instance, has relied on a concept of a quality-adjusted life-year metric that is used to settle on the value of a patient's life relative to the cost of the drug. This is clearly not an acceptable formula applicable in the United States. The Orphan Drug Act mandates that payment must be made in all cases. But there is, nevertheless, the need for a more analytic approach to deciding on the cost effectiveness of a drug.

A solution lies in considering not just the cost of the drug, but in improving its efficacy relative to that cost, (a good proxy for measuring value). Orphan diseases have indications, and if a drug covers it, then insurers must cover it. But this does not help in ascertaining if patients in fact have that orphan status code. The physician is responsible for verifying and submitting it on a claim form and certifies that the patient has it. Then insurance companies can screen the claim and refuse payment unless the screen is met. This critical element—evidence of substantiation—is the leverage point upon which the decision is made.

The issue here is that the industry needs to have better biomarkers for orphan diseases. As biomarkers are discovered that have promise as an indicator for a particular disease, they need to be validated. But many of the orphan diseases are genetically based. As progress has been made in the ability of science to create subsets on the biology of man, we are becoming more refined and are better able to target a homogenous subset of diseases that meet the mathematical definition of an orphan disease. But the issue is that there is often a conflict between the definition of a disease, and the ability to make a clean diagnosis of a specific orphan condition. Evidence of this is our movement to the *International Classification of Diseases* (ICD10) and the likelihood of an ICD11 in the next five years.

The problem with the current reimbursement and manufacturing model is that it is essentially a retail product–based model. Someone has a drug for sale, and the patient wants to buy it through the agent (pharmacy) and distributor, and to make it more affordable there is an insurance industry. This is a product-focused approach that spreads the risk, which has created an inflection point that is unsustainable. The technology of genetic DNA is forcing a change in this product- and transaction-oriented environment and how we manage healthcare. This brings us to our vision for the future.

First, manufacturers of orphan drugs need to provide greater cost transparency for auditing purposes. They should also be more open on their technology roadmap for R&D investments, to targeting orphan diseases that are high in terms of the probability of successful outcomes, and the size of orphan disease populations.

This, in turn, leads to a second issue. Manufacturers should be prepared to provide comparative cost effectiveness (CCE) analytical models for an orphan drug to payers, and to provide clear data supporting the decision for insurance payers, who will be able to judge the value of these high-cost/low-distribution drugs much more clearly. The research suggests insurance companies do not have the internal resources for CCE measurement, analysis of data, and that the same old strategy of increasing tiered payments further is nonproductive. This is an important area for further development.

Finally, the early integration of insurance payer medical and pharmacy boards into the manufacturer clinical trials study design can also help to derive biomarkers and other key indicators that can help to target patients more quickly and identify those who will have clinical benefit from the medicine.

Today's research organizations in preclinical studies are primarily engaged in understanding how to treat or manage diseases. Occasionally, a drug is discovered that can actually cure a disease, but this is exceptionally rare. When a target is identified, it is moved into a clinical phase where animals and humans go through clinical trials to derive empirical evidence of the drug's safety and efficacy. Nowhere in this process is there any evidence of a discussion of target costs, payer requirements, patient preferences, or ability to pay. The assumption is that if we produce a medication that is associated with an orphan drug indicator, they will have to pay. Manufacturers will also need to begin thinking through not only the targeted populations for efficacy, but also how the drug will be administered, delivered, and complied with to be effective.

COMPARATIVE COST-EFFECTIVENESS MODELS

Comparative cost-effectiveness analytical methods hold promise as a potential solution where insurers and manufacturers can collaborate to identify targeted drugs that are not only maximal in their efficacy, but whose costs can be covered. For example, Medco recently acquired Generation Help, and CVS Caremark has a biomarker in the molecular diagnostics space. Some pharmacy benefits managers are beginning to invest in biomarker capabilities to do more sophisticated testing and personalized medicine. Simply relying on the formulary as the instrument for cost effectiveness is unlikely to be productive, and only scratches the surface of what true cost effectiveness needs to be.

While this is an admirable goal, the quality and availability of comparative cost evidence is thin, not because of a lack of trying. Indeed, the Patient-Centered Outcomes Research Institute (PCORI)[*] was authorized by Congress to conduct research to provide information about the best available evidence to help patients and their healthcare providers make more informed decisions. Their primary mission is to provide patients a better understanding of the prevention, treatment, and care options available, and the science that supports those options. This is to be achieved by:

- Assessing the benefits and harms of preventive, diagnostic, therapeutic, palliative, or health delivery system interventions to inform decision making, highlighting comparisons and outcomes that matter to people;

[*] PCORI. http:// www.pcori.org

- Including an individual's preferences, autonomy, and needs, focusing on outcomes that people notice and care about such as survival, function, symptoms, and health-related quality of life;
- Incorporating a wide variety of settings and diversity of participants to address individual differences and barriers to implementation and dissemination; and
- Investigating optimizing outcomes while addressing burden to individuals, availability of services, technology, and personnel, and other stakeholder perspectives.

One of the major challenges that exist is the lack of a standardized approach for conducting CCE research. This was clearly articulated in the words of one manufacturer we interviewed during the course of this research.

Rarely have I been able to cite a peer-reviewed source that supports our argument for my brands that has been agreed on or supported by health plans. "Those aren't my patients" is a typical response. The U.S. does not have a NICE like in the UK that provides a centralized approach for judging health outcomes. It is not my intention to surprise insurance providers and PBMs [pharmacy benefit managers]. In fact, I meet with them to provide pipeline reviews and line of sight to products that are 18 to 20 months away. Surprising the actuaries, health policy people, and finance directors does not produce viable long-lasting relationships. But what troubles health plans is that medicines go from current palliative treatments to curative medicines that are cost dense. And these medicines often get put behind a long list of generic alternatives. So my only hope for an orphan drug is to demonstrate that in a subpopulation is has better efficacy and efficiency which adds a level of precision, so that we no longer have to compete with generics.

These approaches will require a very different approach than the antagonistic model that exists today in the healthcare supply chain. What is needed is a broader network of independent research laboratories that is able to conduct targeted research independent from manufacturers or insurance providers. For example, agencies such as the Agency for Healthcare Research and Quality, the BCBS Chicago Technology Assessment Center, and the National Pharmacy Council should be relied on to carry out this work. And finally, a stronger methodological approach is also required.

TALENT AND COMPETENCY DEVELOPMENT

Today's physician is hardly technology savvy. Walk into a typical physician's office, and the first thing you see is a filing cabinet holding tens of thousands of patient files. Now imagine what the filing cabinet of a major hospital looks like. Similarly, it seems like every time you walk in, you need to complete a HIPPA form, which is typically photocopied with half of the writing blurred from being copied multiple times.

This environment, by definition, will have to change as providers and payers move into the world of network integration. We are starting to see physicians who are seeing patients with laptops and iPads, as well as computers in offices that are linking patient records into a computer. Nurses will often review your medications at a visit into a computer file, which is then printed out and handed to a doctor or intern who visits with you next.

One of the most important elements for organizations to adopt in their evolutionary network model involves understanding the ability to drive learning when systems and activities are in motion. For example, one of the prized attributes identified by many organizations is *learning agility*. One biopharmaceutical company we worked with has made learning agility a formal element in their leadership assessments.

A major characteristic of successful people at any level and age is being a learner—actively making sense of work and personal experiences, adding those lessons to their lifelong learnings portfolio, and striving to get better. In multi-year studies at the Center for Creative Leadership (CCL), one of the glaring differences between successful executives and those whose careers, although successful in the early years, go into eclipse (they derail) is their agility in wrestling meaning from experience. Successful executives are much more likely to have active and numerous learning strategies. They learn faster, gaining their lessons closer to on-the-spot, not because they are more intelligent, but because they have more learning skills and strategies that help them learn what to do when they don't know what to do. They are also more open to what they don't know. They are energized by the challenge of learning how to do something better and differently. In contrast, less successful managers tend to learn randomly or not at all. Their lessons either form no pattern or are vague pronouncements without much meat to them. They are not active learners who seek to make sense of their experiences, searching for learning that might be applicable in the future. They are not energized by knowing something.*

In the next two to five years, I expect that we will start to see team building and technology fluency introduced into medical schools, as well as basic classes in cost management and accounting. This seems contradictory to many codes in the medical profession, but the fact is that physicians will have to become much more capable of working in a networked environment in the future. Ten years from now, we may see team building and technology analytics as part of the provider operating environment, with regular council meetings of physicians, payers, providers, and manufacturers evaluating data, adopting new technologies for improving patient outcomes, and discussing lessons learned from previous therapeutic data collected over time. Eventually, there may even be direct social media communications between physicians, patients, and therapeutic services affiliated with manufacturers around how best to decide on dosage, therapeutic programs, and personalized medicine. This is already the case in hemophilia, where real-time interaction of clinical decisions with service providers is occurring.

The move to a networked culture is indeed going to bring many changes ahead.

_____

THE IMPETUS FOR CHANGE

Our experience is that many physicians and healthcare executives are afraid of change. The problem is that once many of them see the need for change, it may be too late. The idea of changing models and bringing nonhealthcare practices into healthcare requires courage and leadership. In my experience, and in the experience of many of my colleagues, a systematic lack of courage to make decisions is the fundamental problem that underlies healthcare provider reform. Many directors of materials management go to conferences and talk about change—but that's where it ends.

A few entities have developed the courage for change. For example, Orlando Health completely reformed their approach to materials

_____

* Robert Lombardo and Michael Eichinger, Learning Agility as a Prime Indicator of Potential. *Human Resource Planning* 27, no. 4 (2004): 12–15.

management, and rejected the system of group purchasing organizations (GPOs), choosing instead to manage their own spend, and drive to a self-distribution system. This entity became a center for cultural change, and allowed their supply chain organization to become much more involved in the operating room (OR) and their own SCM processes, including the pharmacy. In all such cases, the imperative is coming from the chief executive officer (CEO) and chief financial officer (CFO), who are seeing the net impact on their bottom line. Unfortunately, the directors and vice presidents of materials management in healthcare are *not* the change agents. Because most healthcare CEOs don't know the opportunities, materials managers are not good at educating them. Instead, they prefer to continue to pursue the only thing they know how to do—squeeze suppliers for price reductions without adopting a significant posture for structural change in their organization. There needs to be a separation of acute and nonacute care, and strategies built around specific suppliers and partners handled on an individual basis with differential value drivers, but a common contract support structure. These are alien concepts to 95% of materials managers in healthcare today. In fact, significantly more progress has been made in the United Kingdom, where change has been much more positive. U.S.-based healthcare providers need to change rapidly and in a disruptive fashion, or risk collapsing into bankruptcy and subquality patient care.

3

Healthcare Reform and the Provider Challenges Ahead

I have been trying to put together sessions for CEOs [chief executive officers] at major healthcare providers to begin thinking about how to handle the difficult times ahead. We have established pilot programs for different associations—and in each case, the CEOs decided not to come and, instead, sent their supply chain directors. These directors are the same people that go to all of the standard meetings. They spend all of the training money going to the same conferences, and it is the same people—and nothing ever happens after they leave the conference. It is the same view of the supply chain, and they keep hoping that it will get better. But the news only gets worse, and still they do nothing. There is very little interest in succession management, or how they should be training the next generation of healthcare executives to deal with the coming storm. And even the organizations that put on the educational programs view academics as competitors who will eat up their members' budgets for learning new ways of operating the supply chain.

One of the sore points is around understanding hospital spend. We have been looking at charge master and item master and other simple methods of understanding spend management. If you think of these as the basic data repositories for making decisions, they provide a basis upon which to begin conducting cost accounting, which could someday provide guidance in building insight into bundled payments. And when you start talking about bundled payments and accountable care organizations [ACOs] the first thing that becomes apparent is that there needs to be a lot more integration. But these guys are still adopting a silo transactional view! No one is thinking about how to integrate our competencies across the network system and tie them to clinical outcomes. Somehow, the two pieces need to come together!

But that means being able to make a link between the patient and clinical performance. If that is to happen, we need to think about the metrics that might drive backward into the system all the way to manufacturers, and understand how that linkage can occur, and the components of building that. How does the supply chain contribute to outcomes, risks, recalls, and clinical performance? How do you measure that?

—Gene Schneller

Professor of Healthcare Management, Arizona State University

Gene's comments illustrate just how bad things have gotten, and how little understanding there is of the maelstrom that lies ahead. Not only are executives stunned like the proverbial deer in the headlights given the enormity of what lies ahead, but leadership to take on change is sorely lacking.

The environment facing providers entering into 2014 are so massive, so complex, and so forbidding, that executives in this industry are simply inert. That is the best description for the state of the industry as I have been able to discern over this past two-to-three years.

This challenge to take on what is now recognized as a sea change in the industry was referred to by Atul Gawande, who delivered the commencement address at Harvard Medical School in 2011. He noted that "We are at a cusp point in medical generations. Not only are doctors of former generations lamenting what the practice has become, but these complaints are symptoms of a deeper condition—which is the reality that medicine's complexity has exceeded our individual capabilities as doctors."[*]

In order to develop an insight into the nature of this complexity, we delve into the conundrums of healthcare provider supply chain characteristics in this chapter. We then return to the idea of what is required to drive change in this environment, and the new role for physicians.

OUTLOOK FOR HEALTHCARE PROVIDERS

In the current healthcare operating environment, the financial health of hospitals is showing an alarming trend, as operating margins are shrinking at a rapid rate. In the last three years, the median operating margin of hospitals continued a three-year slide to 1.5% in 2008

---

[*] Atul Gawande, "Cowboys and Pit Crews," *The New Yorker*, March 26, 2011. p. 32. http:\\www.newyorker.com/onlineblogs/newsdesk/2011/os/atul-gawande-harvard-medical-school-commencement-address.html

compared with 2.1%, 2.5%, and 2.8% in 2007, 2006, and 2005, respectively.* In 2008, 29% of hospitals lost money on operations. Finally, according to new statistics from the American Hospital Association, the nation's 5,010 nonfederal community hospitals posted a $17 billion overall profit in fiscal 2008, down 61% from the previous year, amid a punishing recession that caused a $20.5 billion reversal in hospitals' investment portfolios.

In light of these alarming facts, healthcare system CEOs are recognizing that a new operating model comprising a new set of competencies is required to be successful in the marketplace. Faced with a need to improve operating margin, there are three possible options for CEOs: (a) increase revenue through service line expansion, (b) reduce nonclinical and clinical full-time employees to cut payroll costs, or (c) understand supply chain cost drivers and optimize spending on external labor and supplies in medical and nonmedical related areas.

For more progressive healthcare providers and hospital systems, the latter category has become a key focus area for mitigating risk and improving operating margin. While many companies have sought to target a reduction in prices paid through volume leveraging agreements with group purchasing organizations (GPOs), the fact is that many of the costs associated with sourcing services and high-cost technologies do not lie in the realm of volume leveraging. As a point of reference, the majority of a typical hospital's spend with third-party suppliers are in services, not medical supplies. Furthermore, a hospital's expenditures with third-party suppliers is generally the second-largest cost component for a hospital after salary, wages, and benefits. For example, as shown below, a major healthcare IDN discovered that as much as 40% of its costs were in third-party supplies and services. Of this amount, roughly 25%–30% was in purchased services. Furthermore, approximately 40%–60% of total supply costs consist of physician and clinically sensitive preference items. These include categories such as:

- Cardiac pacemaker generators or implantable defibrillators or accessories
- Joint replacement implants
- Neurosurgical and spine implants

---

* Melanie Evans, "Moody's Report Shows Margins Slid in 2008," *Modern Healthcare*, http://www.modernhealthcare.com/article/20090828/NEWS/308289934#, August 28, 2009.

- Coronary stents
- Orthopedic trauma implants
- Cardiothoracic implants
- Human tissue implants
- Diagnostic or interventional vascular catheters or sets
- Electrosurgical or electrocautery equipment or accessories
- Cardiac pacing leads, electrodes, accessories

In the context of this chapter, we define four primary groups:

- **Hospital Operations:** Chief executive officers, chief financial officers, and chief operations officers responsible for directing and leading the hospital/hospital system.
- **Physicians/healthcare providers:** Clinicians who work in operating rooms, intensive care units (ICUs), oncology, or other specific hospital units. These individuals are in direct contact with patients.
- **Supply Chain:** Chief procurement officer, supply chain directors, buyers, analysts, and other individuals who work directly in managing the supply chain for externally provided third-party materials and services. The supply chain should be the major conduit to the supplier community.
- **Suppliers:** Providers of all forms of third-party products and services, including not only clinical materials, but hospital maintenance, transportation, cafeteria services, janitorial, and other indirect products and services that are not used in a clinical environment but are critical to running a hospital.

We begin by introducing some of the major challenges that lie ahead in the regulation and pay-for-performance and bundled payments environment for hospitals. We next demonstrate how completely incapable hospitals are in terms of their level of preparation for these changes. This is achieved by first introducing a healthcare supply chain maturity model that documents the journey that all firms travel, regardless of industry, and show why healthcare is in the nascent stages of this journey. Next, we explore the diversity of perspectives that is at the root of the failure of healthcare to move forward. Specifically, we examine the diversity of objectives that exist among physicians, administrators, supply chain managers, and suppliers. Next, we illustrate through the application of a case study, one approach that proved to be successful in resolving this dilemma. We conclude with the implications for future improvement in the healthcare arena.

CHALLENGES ON THE HORIZON FOR BIOPHARMACEUTICAL COMPANIES IN THE HOSPITAL PROVIDER ENVIRONMENT

Personalized Medicine and Pay for Performance

Attending the IDN Summit in Phoenix on September 13, 2011, one wouldn't know, judging by the relaxed atmosphere at the beautiful Arizona Biltmore, that there was an underlying tension in the air. At this meeting of hospital supply chain executives, there was a growing realization that massive changes in the reimbursement structure for hospital payments was about to occur. There were several big themes that dominated the conversation, and number one on that list was the Accountable Care Act of 2010, which contains over $155 billion in hospital payment cuts over ten years. As part of the reform law, a new Hospital Inpatient Value-Based Purchasing Program begins soon, with 2% of Medicare payments at risk by 2016.

What is the concern? The biggest issue is a new measure of hospital quality, called *Medicare spending per beneficiary*, which will penalize higher-cost hospitals under a formula that could take away far more than value-based purchasing. In this environment, supply chain groups are being called upon to expand their purview into areas once reserved solely for physicians and clinicians—surgery, cardiac catheterization, imaging, and others. But many clinical departments have legacy systems for inventory or no systems at all, which means performance measurement is a challenge for them.

Reimbursement Models

Payers are using a lot of tools to control the overall cost of biologics and new drugs in hospital therapy and are establishing a number of different restrictions in reimbursing drugs. Some of the major categories[*] are discussed next.

---

[*] Rjaram Iver, "Changing Market Access Strategies in Pharmaceutical Industry," Ananth Consulting Group, White Paper, August 2010.

Pay for Performance

This involves a negotiated agreement between the life sciences company and the payer, in which reimbursement is based on the performance of the drug for individual payments. This approach has its origins in pay for performance. Examples include the agreement between the United Kingdom's National Health Service (NHS) and Johnson & Johnson for an oncology drug, Velcade. Under this agreement, the NHS will only pay if the Velcade treatments demonstrate a desired response measured by the reduction in tumor size.* Another example is the agreement between the National Institute for Clinical Excellence in the United Kingdom and Novartis for Lucentis, an eye treatment. Novartis agreed to cover the cost of treatment if more than fourteen injections are required for ongoing treatment of the patient.

The United Stated is also focusing on pay-for-performance (PFP) measures. This has already occurred with Aetna and Cigna, who have a lot of PFP partnerships with a number of hospitals. In August 2006, Aetna launched a national PFP program under which it incentivizes physicians who improve the quality of care and reduce the overall treatment cost. This is also part of a broader program aimed at reducing the cost of payments for biologics and drugs bundled with physician fees, to drive to a *bundled payment* outcome.

Step Edit Therapy

This tool has also been applied for a number of years and poses a threat to the life sciences industry and healthcare providers alike. In this approach, a typically less-expensive or generic version of a drug is authorized first before another drug (e.g., the more expensive branded drug) can be authorized for use. The branded, new drug is authorized only when the earlier generic, less-expensive version has been shown to be ineffective. Step edit is popular in countries where generics proliferate. Most payers in the United States use this approach for various therapies, but especially so in the case of biologics-based therapies.

Examples of step edit therapy include the case of Blue Cross of Idaho, which imposed a step edit on Byetta, a new medication for diabetes. Based on the guidelines, Byetta is placed on a third tier of approved formulary

---

* National Institute for Health and Clinical Excellence (NICE), http://ec.europa.eu/enterprise/sectors/healthcare/files/docs/risksharing_oncology_0120_11_en.pdf.

drugs, and is only authorized when patients have taken at least two other agents or one combination drug with no effect.* Similarly, the Harvard Pilgrim Health Care program established a step edit on Vyotorin. Patients are encouraged to maximize the statin dose before adding the drug to their regimen.

Price Capping

This payer strategy involves capping the price for various drugs for a particular treatment. Payers fix an upper cap on the reimbursement for a drug used for a particular treatment. This strategy has also been adopted by manufacturers. For example, Genentech capped the total cost of Avastin, a cancer treatment, for the approved indication at $55,000 per year for individuals below a certain income level. Amgen also capped a patient's annual copayment for Vectivix at 5% of the patient's adjusted gross income.

Outcome-Based Pricing

Biopharma companies have seen the writing on the wall and have begun exploring outcome-based risk-sharing arrangements with payers. One example is an outcome-based agreement developed by Janssen-Cilag and the National Institute for Health and Clinical Excellence (NICE) in the United Kingdom. NICE refused to approve the drug based on cost effectiveness, so the company proposed to treat eligible patients for four months, and be paid based on the contingency that patient outcomes result. If the drug achieves a specific response, patients are permitted to continue the treatment and NHS will cover the expense. Otherwise, Janssen must cover the cost and reimburse the NHS for its expenses. In another example, Merck has signed a deal with Cigna whereby Merck's two antidiabetic drugs, Januvia and Janumet, are reimbursed according to their performance. Cigna is seeking to develop a broader set of agreements with statin manufacturers that is pushing the boundaries even further. If the patient suffers from a heart attack taking statins on a regular basis, manufacturers must pay for the treatment cost![†]

---

[*] Iver, Rjarem 2010. Changing Market Access Strategies in Pharmaceutical Industry, White Paper, August 2010. Ananth Consulting Group.

[†] Paul Jones and Jan Malek, "Prospering in a Pay-for-Performance World," white paper, Cisco Systems, Inc.

Accountable Care Organizations

A major trend that is catching many healthcare providers by storm in 2012 is the notion of accountable care organizations (ACO). In the 429-page document developed by the Centers for Medicare and Medicaid Services (CMS), ACOs are defined as organizations whose primary care providers are accountable for coordinating care for at least 5,000 Medicare beneficiaries, as a separate legal entity. These organizations are accountable to provide better care for individuals, better health for populations based on preventive services, and lower growth in expenditures, based on a vague concept called *patient-centeredness*.

This document becomes even more threatening to current operating models for hospitals, as a big chunk of Medicare reimbursement will be tied to something called *comparative effectiveness*. This means that there must be a firmer scientific basis for determining the clinical value and cost–benefit of devices, drugs, and interventions through comparative effectiveness research (CER). This is intended to avoid using technologies that are adopted into practice without sufficient evidence and that have caused harm to patients, including high-dose chemotherapy, drugs like Vioxx, and bone morphogenetic protein, which has a risk of sterility in men. All well and good, except for the fact that there are no databases, lousy performance metrics, and no standards for the protocol or types of diseases and patient characteristics that provide a precedent for measuring whether a treatment is effective or not.

Another looming issue is bundled payments. Under this format, a provider is no longer paid in terms of a fee for service while a patient is in the hospital. In a fee-for-service model, each member of the medical team—the radiologist, the cardiologist, the anesthesiologist, and perhaps the consulting physician who works with the patient afterward (as well as the life sciences company providing the medical therapy)—is paid separately based on their activity. In bundled payments, a single fee is charged for the entire procedure, including possible readmission fees for up to thirty–ninety days after the patient is discharged. Combine this with the fact that Medicare payments today are about 50% of hospital revenues and that in five years they may be as high as 90% of revenues!

So how this all comes together is that ACOs are required to implement evidence-based medicine. This means hospitals are to be held accountable not only for the cost of the care they provide, but for the cost of services performed by doctors and other healthcare providers in the thirty days after a Medicare patient leaves the hospital.

There is also an impending conflict between the two schools of thought that represent CER and personalized medicine (PM) views on the effectiveness of different biological and pharmaceutical treatments on patients. The purpose of both methods involves seeking to support high-quality, evidence-based decisions for optimal patient care. The difference lies in the fact that CER is oriented toward evaluating treatment effects across study populations, while PM focuses on using individuals' genomic information and other personal traits to inform decisions about their healthcare.[*]

What this means is that CER does not investigate important differences in patient response to interventions, (for example, whether patient response to a cancer drug varies by certain genetic characteristics), because its findings may be inadequate or misleading for patient care. This could have extended consequences if these findings are incorporated into product labeling, practice guidelines, reimbursement policies, or utilization management that could curtail PM.

For CER to contribute to PM, it must account for patient differences that influence the impact of interventions on health outcomes. These characteristics can include severity of disease, comorbidities and risk factors, genetic characteristics, sociodemographic characteristics, health-related behaviors, environmental factors, and more.

Aligning CER and PM means that PM is subject to prevailing evidence requirements for screening, diagnostic, therapeutic, and other interventions. For genetic and genomic testing, health professional groups, guideline panels, and payers are calling not only for rigorous evidence of test accuracy, but for evidence of clinical utility, that is, impact of test results on clinical decisions, and ultimately patient outcomes. This applies, for example, to gene expression profile testing to predict breast cancer outcomes, pharmacogenomic testing for guiding treatment for depression, and selecting treatments for colorectal cancer.

REGULATORY FORECAST FOR HEALTHCARE REFORM

Healthcare reform is the massive game changer that is looming on the horizon. Every senior executive in the life sciences and in any discipline of

---

[*] Michael McCaughan, "Can Personalized Medicine and Comparative Effectiveness Coexist? The Experts Weigh In," *The RPM Report* 9, no. 10 (2009).

healthcare needs to be closely tracking the changes that are afoot, as the debate is no longer *will it happen* but *how much change* will occur? Every entity in the life sciences needs to meet the challenges of the new delivery models, reimbursement shifts, increased scrutiny, and restrictions that are afoot in the patient network channel. The context of this chapter and this discussion is based on insights from several senior legal representatives speaking at the IDN Summit in October 2011, and represent an honest assessment of what lies ahead.

The historical struggle between quality clinical outcomes and the need to meet financial goals is giving way to a new era where high-quality patient care brings with it financial reward, and meaningful data analysis can help to bridge the gap between supply chain and quality care objectives. This evolution spurs the desire for new methods of aligning financial goals with clinical ones to maximize synergies.

Achieving a clinically integrated supply chain is a journey relying on strong value analysis and evidence-based practices. Engaging physicians and management, and the use of data and other means of evaluating product selection and utilization will play key roles. Another important component of capability involves gathering intelligence, gleaning actionable data through service line analytics, and building solution strategies that lay the groundwork for adjusting to bundled payments without sacrificing patient outcomes.

Evidence-Based Medicine (EBM): The Foundation for Pay for Performance

Evidence-based medicine dates back to the mid-nineteenth century in Paris and later arrived in the United States after World War II. Prior to that time, medicine was primarily a means to manage pain and disease, but without any real scientific basis for making decisions. Evidence-based medicine is the "conscientious explicit and judicious use of current best evidence in making decisions about the care of individual patients."[*] This essentially means "using individual clinical expertise and the best available external evidence, in an integrated fashion, to make clinical decisions about the care of an individual patient."[†]

---

[*] D. L. Sachett, W. M. Rosenberg, J. J. Gray, R. B. Haynes, and W. S. Richardson, "Evidence Based Medicine: What It Is and What It Isn't," *British Medical Journal* 312 (1986): 22.

[†] Neil Olderman, "Moving toward Greater Accountability in Evidenced-Based Medicine," presentation at IDN Summit, Phoenix, AZ, September 16, 2011.

While this seems relatively straightforward as a definition, the legal challenge occurs due to the potential for conflict of interest. The decision-making process used in medicine involves the physician formulating a clear clinical question from a patient's problem, searching relevant clinical literature for articles, evaluating the evidence for validity and usefulness, and implementing useful findings for specific patients based on their particular circumstances, as well as the patient's individual preferences. In effect, there is no "single cookbook" approach to treating a patient. The focus is on the patient's state, their specific predicament, and their individual preferences as to how they want to treat the problem. The physician's skill involves weighing all of these issues, and applying them in the most efficacious manner, which means that not all patients will be treated the same way. It is also clear that cost is one of several factors used in decision making. The objective is to identify and apply the most efficient interventions to maximize the quality and quantity of life for individual patients. And this is where it becomes complicated, because there must be some form of cost-effectiveness research or a comparative effectiveness dataset against which to derive a decision. Another way of depicting this is as a *total cost model*, which identifies the cost of treatment, the probability of success, and the total cost over the life of the patient.

The problem, of course, is not as simple as it is depicted here, because there is ample opportunity for conflicts of interest to occur in the decision-making process. First, randomized controlled trials (RCTs) are universally accepted as the most useful form of analysis and comparison for EBM. The results of RCTs published in a medical journal are the most common way of demonstrating the efficacy and safety of a particular medicine or treatment. The process, when done appropriately, is a meticulous scientific analysis that provides physicians and patients some level of comfort in selecting a treatment. However, the legal community has dissected published RCT studies and has found that multiple potential conflicts of interest exist, particularly for the biopharmaceutical industry, which poses questions as to the integrity of the results of RCTs.

Critics[*] of evidence-based medicine have described the system of scientific research and publication as "broken." They point to unethical practices that include the suppression of negative data, ghostwriting, disease mongering, market segmentation, and lack of accountability. This

---

[*] G. I. Spielman and P. I. Parry, 2010 "From Evidence-Based Medicine to Market-Based Medicine: Evidence from Internal Industry Documents," *Bioethical Inquiry* 7, no. 1 (2010): 13–29.

is not to say that ties among physicians, researchers, and industry are not common, or that widespread relationships have improved individual and public health. However, it is true that the media has focused on the negative on high-profile instances of conflicts, such as a lack of transparency of financial relations among researchers and manufacturers, conflict of interest among authors of research studies, illegal payments or gifts, failure to disclose substantial payments, or delay of publication of negative results.[*] In general, however, the research on conflict of interest is inconclusive as to the impact of financial relationships between physicians and industry.[†] There are no systematic studies, and while the data are suggestive, they are certainly not definitive and are primarily observational in nature. There is also a lot of diversity in the extent to which conflict of interest policies are enforced among institutions. So there is a bifurcation among the experts— some say it is worse than noted, and some say it is not as bad as published.

The biggest problem with evidence-based medicine; however, goes beyond potential conflict-of-interest issues—there is no single source of truth and no monopoly on interpreting data and studies. There are middlemen, aggregators, and others that give physicians a lot of information. Doctors don't have time to read all the articles and do the research on their own and have to rely on these sources for their information. The government is trying to propose a solution for this (discussed later). Consumer beliefs about EBM add another layer of complexity to the issue. Consumers typically want a pill when they go to the doctor and have an idea that every ill can be cured using a medical "cookbook." Even if evidence shows that medicine will not cure a patient's problem, consumers always believe that their access to medicine is being restricted if they are denied their request. Consumers also believe in the following often incorrect tenets: (1) medical guidelines are inflexible and not appropriate to impose, (2) more care and newer care is better, (3) more expensive care is better, and (4) challenging a physician is unacceptable behavior. For this reason, *Health Affairs* points out that consumers are skeptical of evidence-based healthcare, and they believe that more expensive care is always better.[‡]

---

[*] Source: Institute of Medicine, Committee on Conflict of Interest in Medical Research, Education and Practice; B. Lo, M.J. Field, editors, National Academies Press, 2009.

[†] G.I. Spielman and P.I. Parry, 2010.

[‡] K. L. Carman, M. Maurer, J. M. Yegian, P. Dardess, J. McGee, M. Evers, and K. O. Marlo, "Evidence that Consumers Are Skeptical about Evidence-Based Health Care," *Health Affairs* 29, no. 7 (2010): 1400–1406.

With the coming of health reform, the U.S. government believed that the general populace needed an extra layer of protection against conflict-of-interest issues. Specifically, Section of 6002 of the Patient Protection and Affordable Care Act (PPACA) focuses on transparency reports, and reporting of physician ownership or investment (the "Physician Sunshine Act") is in the works. This legislation applies to manufacturers and GPOs that transfer value to covered recipients (physicians and teaching hospitals). It requires the reporting of physician ownership or investment in academic or private institutions and requires physicians to disclose financial relationships. Even though reporting is due March 31, 2015, it was effective January 1, 2012, and must cover payments and other investments. Reports must include charitable giving, consulting fees, compensation, education, entertainment, food, gifts, grants, honoraria, investment interests, and so on. This impacts all healthcare providers.

This leads to the next major issue—CER, which first received attention in the 2009 Economic Stimulus. At that time, $1.1 billion was allocated for research grants and investment in research tools, methodologies, and infrastructure (e.g., patient databases) to support reliable research. Subtitle D, Section 6301 of the PPACA made permanent a national Comparative Effectiveness Research Program, which was subsequently given the incongruous title of the Patient-Centered Outcome Research Institute (PCORI).

PCORI is an independent not-for-profit organization, funded with federal stimulus dollars initially, and fees imposed by federal law on health insurers and self-funded employer plans. It is governed by a twenty-one-member board, which includes two members from the federal or state government, seventeen members from outside government appointed by the U.S. comptroller general, and two seats for the directors of the Agency for Health Care Research and Quality (AHRQ) and the National Institutes of Health (NIH). Federal employees are not compensated, but board members are.

This is not a government agency, but is chartered by federal law and empowered to assist patients, clinicians, purchasers, and policy makers in making informed decisions by:

- Advancing the quality and relevance of evidence about prevention, management, and treatment options
- Synthesizing research and evidence that considers variations in patient subpopulations

- Disseminating research findings concerning relative health outcomes, clinical effectiveness, and appropriateness of treatments, services, and items

It will establish an agenda, set requirements for publication, have access to Medicare data, and appoint expert advisory panels. All of those activities will be required. But it is not yet clear how this will be accomplished.

PCORI is obligated to ensure transparency, credibility and access, and provide for public comment on national agendas, methodological standards, peer-review processes, and drafts of systematic reviews of research.

It is also important to note the limitations on the use of CER. One of the most important elements is that Center for Medicare and Medicaid Services (CMS) is prohibited from using research to make Medicare coverage decisions unless it is "through an interactive and transparent process." This means that CMS will have access to the information, and use it to make decisions, through a process that is open and transparent. There is no doubt that there will be financial coverage decisions based on PCORI information.

The conflict-of-interest burden of responsibility for healthcare providers begins in January 2012, and behavior will have to change. Conflict-of-interest disclosure and reporting will require much more intensive focus and commitment to compliance and training. The coming health reform will also highlight the need for reliable and high-quality medical evidence because PCORI (even though a nongovernmental, board-run organization) will have broad authority to impact the industry. Its specific impact at the moment is unknown.

Providers thus need to begin to work with biopharmaceutical companies to begin to develop a posture toward CER, and how aggressive or passive they will be in establishing the standards of care and the evidence that is used to shape decisions. There is no doubt that traditional methods of research and publication will continue, but life sciences organizations need to begin building a strategic intent toward their level of involvement. This is a good time to be at the table. This means that industry members should begin to dedicate the time to monitor PCORI meetings, attend hearings, and coordinate with industry and patient advocacy groups on initiatives. Most importantly, biopharma must work with providers to make public comments available including research supportive of specific treatments, products, devices, or processes. Some of the public forums to monitor and participate in include the Institute of Medicine of the National Academies (http://iom.edu) and the New England Healthcare Institute (http://www.nehi.net).

Accountable Care Organizations (ACOs)*

As we've noted, electronic collaboration and information sharing of patient information between providers isn't a common attribute found in healthcare systems, making it difficult to diagnose and track the efficacy of medicines. Accountable care organizations hold out the promise of being able to do this, but there is also considerable confusion surrounding the term *ACO*. What does it really mean? Is there such a thing as nonaccountable care versus accountable care?

An ACO refers to a group of providers and suppliers of services that will work together to coordinate care for the patients they serve with original Medicare. The goal of an ACO is to deliver seamless high-quality care for beneficiaries. They are like the elusive unicorn, everyone knows what it looks like, but no one has actually seen one. More specifically, an ACO is a type of payment and delivery reform model that starts to tie provider reimbursements to quality metrics and reductions in the total cost of care for an assigned population of patients. A group of coordinated healthcare providers form an ACO, which then provides care to a group of patients. Federal officials believe ACOs could save Medicare up to $960 million in the next three years.

The "drop-dead date" was October 1, 2012, when Medicare instituted the national hospital value-based purchasing (VBP) program mandated by the PPACA. A VBP score is calculated based on the quality of outcomes. Recently, a national analysis of hospital performance by VHA Inc[†]. calculated a national median VBP score of 53, when hospitals likely will need scores higher than 70 to maximize their Medicare reimbursements. The median risk for VPB loss is $250,000 for 2012 for hospitals, and $1.88 million over five years. To avoid these losses, the biggest cost savings in future reimbursement models comes from keeping patients out of hospitals, which in turn reduces hospital revenues. This is an incredible paradox.

Although viewed as a threat by healthcare executives, ACOs are actually well-intentioned. Today we are stuck with a siloed and fragmented system,

---

[*] Joel Sangerman, Payer Relations Director, DePuy Mitek, "Clinical Pharmacy—Business Innovation," presentation at the IDN Summit, Phoenix, AZ, September 2011.

[†] Joel Sangerman, 2011. "Clinical Pharmacy-Business Innovation," Presentation at the Integrate Distribution Network (IDN) Summit, Phoenix, Arizona, September 2011.

and uncoordinated care. A recent study found that 13% of patients sixty or older had to have tests redone, 36% received conflicting information, and 76% left a physician's office or hospital confused about what to do next in their care.

By 2017, $857 billion in healthcare spending will be under the new healthcare reform act provisions. To complicate matters, 96% of spending in 2017 will be on patients with four or more chronic conditions, and who may be seeing as many as five–eleven different physicians. So an ACO can reduce the amount of duplication of services, mitigate the high cost of out-of-network providers, develop better transition strategies, and provide better information sharing. From a financial perspective, the mix of private to government healthcare spending is approximately at a 50/50 split, but by 2030, 75% of a hospital's payer mix will be Medicare or Medicaid, which is a recipe for bankruptcy of the economy.

Another reason for the need for ACOs is that there are too many beneficiaries with multiple conditions and multiple physicians who don't share results, which in turn leads to medical mistakes and too many patient discharges that result in readmission in thirty days or fewer.

There are several ACO payment methods that are on the horizon. The first of these is called *pay for performance* or by the other moniker *value-based purchasing*, which means payment is based on compliance with certain outcomes and performance metrics. Another payment approach is *bundled payments*, which are an attempt to bundle all of the services associated with an acute care project and price it under a single price tag. This means taking the physician services from physician A, physician B, and so on, and creating a single diagnosis-related group (DRG) with a single payment, which is then divided among these providers. There are proposals to bundle an entire episode of care, including thirty-, sixty-, or ninety-day postdischarge patient care. There may even be a day when health systems can bid for the opportunity to provide a DRG based on different payment policies.

Healthcare Supply Chain Maturity

Schneller and Smeltzer note in their text that the majority of health providers have relatively immature supply chains, and that development of strategic management of supply chains is generally at a nascent level.* One method

---

* E. Schneller and L. R. Smeltzer, *Strategic Management of the Health Care Supply Chain* (San Francisco: John Wiley, 2006).

of depicting the supply chain transformation that occurs in organizations is the maturity model we identified earlier, based on prior research on supply chain maturity.* As shown in Figure 3.1, organizations typically proceed through an evolution of basic processes in supply management. Initially, most providers are not focused on managing the supply chain, but rely on an external GPO to negotiate all of their contracts, and focus on driving compliance in the physician/healthcare worker community. Organizations seeking to drive change must first begin by establishing a charter to do so with their executive team, and make a commitment to moving away from a transaction price–based focus.

In the second level of maturity, supply chain managers begin to engage clinicians in sourcing decisions, particularly high-value and clinically sensitive items. These teams are directed to make decisions on matching value relative to needs, analysis of spending patterns, measurements of supplier performance, and establishing a baseline set of data to analyze trends. However, the most important component of success at this stage is physician and clinical engagement in decision making that explicitly considers patient outcomes and total cost, not just year-over-year product price reductions. In later stages, organizations can move to material and service visibility throughout the supply chain, management of total cost on a systemwide basis, engagement of suppliers in hospital operations, integration of new technology deployment that drives down total cost and improves patient outcomes. The more mature systems are also focused on global or partial capitation (limits) on payments for specific procedures. Electronic health records (EHRs) are leveraged to build profiles on patients, and to employ strategic cost models to begin evaluating different types of medical treatments and reimbursement procedures. Manufacturers begin to collaborate with hospital providers to create comparative cost effectiveness (CCE) analytical models of an orphan drug for payers, and provide clear data supporting decisions for insurance payers, who will be able to judge the value of these high-cost, low-distribution drugs much more clearly.

Where Are Providers on the Maturity Curve? The Broken Venn Relationship

Based on our interviews and analyses of healthcare providers, we observed that many systems are still stuck in the first stage of supply chain

---

* R. B. Handfield, *Supply Market Intelligence* (Boca Raton, FL: Auerbach, 2008).

Network Partners = CMOs, Suppliers, Co-Mfg. Partners, Wholesalers, Retailers, Hospitals, Physicians, Payers, & Patients!				
Initiatives	Ad Hoc No Process	Defined Reactive	Managed/Standard	Leveraged Advanced
Governance	Physician acts independently based on "cowboy" mentality	Internal consultation with other physicians	Regular reviews of options with patients and payers. Preventive care policies. Regular 3rd party engagement	Aligned patients council with key network partners and reporting structure at major decision points
Network Culture	Silo physician culture. Single decisions with little patient or 3rd party review	Process defined & documented Some compliance to payer requirements	Regular patient discussions with payers and providers	Network partners (Suppliers, payers, etc.) engaged in strategic patient reviews
Management Systems & Analytics	Independent patient records	Patient analytics in an Electric Health Record	Physician performance tied to patient outcomes as measured by EHR. Should-cost modeling and total-cost models used to drive payer negotiations and policies	EHR linked to aligned metrics, milestones and contract mgmt. with networked partners by segment. Social media/alternative technologies used to drive transparency
Patient Disease (Risk) Management	Firefighting and mitigation based on appearance of symptoms	Diagnosis based on patient history and monitoring	Biomarkers and genetic analysis provides early warning of potential diseases and preventive medical treatment	Lifelong patient monitoring by third parties with specialized delivery and monitoring through social media
Administering and Deployment of Technologies/Therapies	Hard handover from R&D to Physician	Transition team documents learning and feedback	Multi-provider/payer/physician team approach to evaluate holistically	Early integration of key network partners into therapeutic and technology decisions
Talent Development	Little technology knowledge	Physician team skills introduced into medical schools, along with technological savvy	Team building and technology integration linked with physician professional career path and therapeutic monitoring of patients	Physicians and patients are actively engaged and communicating with biopharma companies through social media
	Current	2–5 years	8–12 years	

FIGURE 3.1

Patient-focused network integration for providers (hospitals, physician offices).

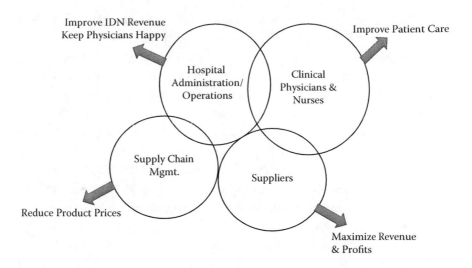

FIGURE 3.2
The current state of most healthcare providers.

maturity. Many do not even have a charter for change established with the C-suite.[*] As noted earlier, many hospital administrators are frustrated by their inability to engage with physicians in supply chain decisions. A typical scenario for decisions often centers on the major gaps that exist among the four major stakeholders in healthcare—hospital operations, physicians, supply chain management, and suppliers. These relationships are best illustrated through the application of a classic Venn diagram, as shown in Figure 3.2. In this diagram, the four diametrically opposed goals of the four key parties are seen to be fundamentally misaligned.

Physician View

There is no question that the majority of physicians are dissatisfied with their current operating environment.[†] The primary modus operandi for physicians in many health systems is to focus on the patient and disregard

---

[*] Robert Handfield, PhD (Bank of America Professor of SCM), Tom Faciszewski MD (orthopedic spine surgeon, Marshfield Clinic, and medical director supply chain, Ministry Health Care), and Thomas Nash, (chief supply chain officer, Ministry Health Care), "Assessing Health Care Supply Chain Maturity: Creating a Baseline for Cost Savings, Value Creation and a Defined Structure for Growth," keynote presentation, World Healthcare Congress, January 25, 2010.

[†] M. Linzer, L. B. Manwell, E. S. Williams, et al., "MEMO (Minimizing Error, Maximizing Outcome) Investigators. Working Conditions in Primary Care: Physician Reactions and Care Quality," *Annals of Internal Medicine* 151, no. 1 (2009): 28–36, W6–9.

any other issues. This is certainly understandable, given that physicians take the Hippocratic Oath, and have been trained throughout their career to be devoted to improving patient care and outcomes. However, a challenge that occurs in this environment is that physicians really don't care about the nuances of supply costs and the supply chain. Physicians generally don't see how hospital operations (suits) or the supply chain (folks in the basement) would ever help them better serve the patient. This observation simply shows that the supply chain business perspective is not a component of physician training, nor are they comfortable with it. Physicians are, however, very familiar with how suppliers can add value to the delivery of patient care and often have deep mutual understandings of this value.

One of the outcomes of this behavior is that physicians often believe they have the right to select medical devices, implants, and maintain personal preference regardless of the cost to the healthcare system. Most often, physicians have not been provided with sufficient information relative to costs and other key factors, and in this vacuum of not having a shared understanding and shared vision, make product decisions based on patient outcomes, their training and comfort level, or preference alone. Many have independent practices, function independently of the financial operations of the hospital, and thus are not aligned directly with hospital profitability or cost, and therefore are left with product familiarity, patient outcomes, and supplier or sales force comfort as the principle rationale for all preference decisions.

This situation is one that must fundamentally change for healthcare reform to occur. Indeed, a recent senior leadership journal noted that "Health Care Needs a New Kind of Hero," that is, physicians who are no longer "cowboys," but who can work as a team with other functions in healthcare.* The challenges that exist for teamwork are covered in the next sections.

Hospital Operations

Not surprisingly, healthcare operations are not aligned on the same issues as physicians or suppliers. And many healthcare operating executives are not familiar with the basic operations management principles that

---

* Interview with Atul Gawande, "Health Care Needs a New Kind of Hero," *Harvard Business Review*, April 2010, 60–61.

the majority of best practice organizations regularly employ to better manage the hospital, such as operations planning, operations research, operations models, and so on. Such principles are now just starting to be understood and applied in healthcare (e.g., lean principles are a perfect example of this). Supplies are viewed essentially as nonnegotiable costs that perhaps can only be negotiated through hardball tactics to drive down price. Many suppliers have a primary goal of keeping physicians happy and driving top-line revenue. Oddly enough, many operations executives do not view the supply chain as a source of bottom-line profitability. The primary role of operations managers in these environments is to do whatever it takes to keep the physicians happy, and try to extract a lower price from suppliers once physicians decide what they want in the operating room (OR) or interventional radiology suite.

Supply Chain Managers

Supply chain managers are often tactically focused, primarily on driving down prices paid through tougher negotiations and command-and-control tactics. One of the overriding trends is that many providers outsource their procurement decisions to GPO, some of whose primary objectives it is to reduce cost by moving large volumes of product to fewer suppliers. The usual end point in this type of model is to have a single source supplier that, in exchange for high contract use compliance, provides substantially reduced pricing. GPOs will then pressure suppliers to extract lower prices and larger supplier rebates or participation fees, regardless of physician preferences. As a result, there is physician resentment and noise, a limited focus on patient outcomes, and little attention paid to indirect costs such as conversion cost, which may be substantial in terms of economic, emotional, and risk to procedure processes in places such as the OR. Additionally, the success of the patient outcomes is not mapped to the different sourcing options.

Linking supply chain performance to bedside patient care and clinical outcomes is often not directly measured or managed; rather, the primary focus is on *price buying* versus *total cost of patient care*. Engagement of key stakeholders, including physicians and suppliers is avoided, and the command-and-control approach to management–physician relationships bogs down change and decision making. Suppliers are also viewed as the enemy, and comparatively little information is provided to them in requests for proposals. Supply risk mitigation (e.g., wrong supply, wrong time, wrong spec, wrong place, etc.) is not very often considered in sourcing decisions, and subsequently there is a limited ability to track relationships among suppliers, technologies, quality, total cost, and patient outcomes. A command-and-control culture dominates, where GPOs wield the club to beat suppliers down, and little collaboration occurs with these same suppliers to identify mutual joint cost-savings opportunities in the operating room, interventional cardiology suite, and other high-cost centers in the hospital.

Suppliers

Given the conflict that exists between physicians and supply chain managers, it is hardly surprising that suppliers avoid any interaction with administrators, and market their products directly to physicians and healthcare workers. Physicians are the suppliers' best allies. Because many physicians have trained on specific devices in medical school and residency, the same suppliers are utilized by the physicians throughout their career, and they are the suppliers' lifeline to the market. Suppliers understand these biases and capitalize on them. By marketing directly to physicians on the basis of improved patient outcomes, price and cost negotiations can easily be avoided with administrators. Not surprisingly, these suppliers are making significant profits as they have been underchallenged. For example, recent studies suggest that research and development costs for the orthopedic device industry are typically 5% of what they are for pharmaceuticals, and that the cost of goods (e.g., materials and production costs) are typically 20% of total price, leaving approximately 75% to cover operating margins, profit, and cost of selling, general, and administrative (SG&A) expenses.[*] The typical hospital operating margin, by comparison, is only 2%, versus 40%–60% for their suppliers.

The broken Venn diagram shown in Figure 3.2 depicts the resulting situation. To summarize, the current operating model in healthcare supply chains is immature, represented by a significant lack of trust among the four parties who have the potential to work together to reduce healthcare cost and improve patient outcomes. Suppliers don't trust administrators, administrators don't trust physicians or suppliers, and physicians don't trust hospitals to make the right decision. There is little to no cooperation, separate

---

[*] Source: Orthopedic Companies, 600bn, available at http://www.600bn.com/?tag=orthopedic-implants, accessed October 2009.

business plans, and very little symbiotic engagement among the parties—and so hospitals continue to lose money and close their doors, and patients and government continue to overpay for surgical procedures and devices.

How did this happen? Why is the system so broken? What can be done to dislodge this culture of lack of trust? In the following case, we explore how one hospital broke the mold and tried something different.

LESSONS LEARNED AND FUTURE DIRECTIONS

There are several important lessons that emerge from our study of health-care supply chains, that are illustrated in the revised Venn diagram shown in Figure 3.3. First of all, it is possible to achieve seemingly diverse objectives for key stakeholders. As shown in Figure 3.3, the core objectives of price competitiveness, total cost reduction, and supply base *rightsizing* can be aligned with physician goals to improve patient outcomes, encourage use of appropriate products, and reduce the variability of the different medical technologies being utilized. By using data in clear and compelling business cases for change to influence physicians of the need for change, supply chain and operations can create solutions that meet aligned goals for all four groups in healthcare. This result isn't uncommon; for instance, Hawthorne Medical Associates uses peer benchmarking, both locally and

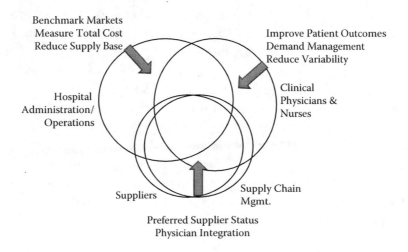

FIGURE 3.3
The collaborative model.

across the network, to drive pay-for-performance measures in areas such as the use of radiology tests. Orders fell by 15% in one group of physicians after they saw how they compared with colleagues on test use.* Second, suppliers, operations, supply chain, or surgeons are not the enemy, but must begin to adopt a more mature approach to a respectful and collaborative influence model, which entails balancing the demands for lower cost and improved patient outcomes, while finding ways to partner more closely to deliver better patient care solutions and be successful in healthcare reform. This is reflected in the fact that the four circles are almost 100% overlapping. In an ideal world, the extended supply chain is highly integrated into operational sourcing decisions, as suppliers are the best resource available. Suppliers bring ideas in the form of value engineering, improvements in technology, and optimized solutions that can take cost out of the supply chain much more effectively than a simple price reduction. Third, the importance of data in a clear and compelling business case for change as a rational and objective means of reaching consensus is made clear in this case. Physicians were not made to *comply* with a proposed solution—they were engaged as part of the solution to reach the collaborative decision that was positive for all involved, most importantly, patient outcomes and affordability. Fourth, healthcare operations must adopt a more proactive and strategic posture toward critical supply categories, and adopt team-based methodologies that are tried and true in most industries, yet are not well developed in most healthcare delivery systems or IDNs.

It should be noted that the lessons illustrated in this project are only the beginning for providers that can create this alignment between groups. Virtually the entire supply base (e.g., suppliers) and the materials and services supplied to the healthcare industry can benefit from more strategic stakeholder engagement (e.g., the influence model) and more sophisticated supply chain management (the "and" model).

The implications of applying world-class supply chain principles to the healthcare environment have the potential to significantly improve the economic viability and patient outcomes for the industry. With annual joint replacement surgery exceeding 700,000 procedures and projected to double by 2016, joint replacement is an important category for application of strategic sourcing approaches. Orthopedic device manufacturers enjoy profits of 70% or more, and medical device suppliers have profits of 60%

---

* Kelly Hall, "Using Peer Pressure to Improve Performance," *Harvard Business Review,* April 2010, 54–55.

or more.* If even a conservative savings of 10% in the joint replacement category could be achieved, a potential savings of $3.5 billion in spending on joint replacement could be achieved across the entire healthcare system. Applied to the broader case of physician preference items, which constitutes approximately 20% of healthcare provider spending, healthcare provider costs could be reduced by as much as 2%–5%, which would effectively double or triple operating margins. With healthcare spending currently at $2.5 trillion, approximately 31% of each dollar spent on healthcare goes to hospital care, and 21% to physician services.† If supply management methodologies are applied to hospital services, a 2%–5% savings would translate to approximately a $15 to $40 billion annual reduction in healthcare spending. We believe that this approach is not only important for the industry in the years ahead, but it is foundational to transformation of healthcare as we know it today.

INTEGRATED DISTRIBUTION NETWORK: JOINT REPLACEMENT CASE STUDY

At this large integrated delivery company a new chief supply chain officer (CSO) was appointed in 2008. This individual was well-versed in the fundamentals of supply management. One of the first tasks was to fully understand the landscape, and in so doing, this individual discovered that cross-functional relationships were very similar to the generic model represented in Figure 3.2. The broken Venn diagram represented the state of relationships in his provider network community. The CSO's first task was to engage operations leadership to support a transition to a strategic supply management orientation, via a solid business case. He shared evidence to show that 30 to 45 cents of every dollar was spent on materials and services, and that in other industries a strategic approach could produce a 3%–7% price improvement alone, and when extended to more mature approaches (as shown in Figure 3.4), could produce a 10%–30% total cost improvement opportunity. With this business case, the IDN invested in supply chain capability, with the expectation of seeing a significant return on investment (ROI). To accomplish this new approach, leaders endorsed

---

* *USA Today*, "Orthopedic Industry Enjoys Fine Health," October 20, 2009.
† Organisation for Economic Co-operation and Development, http://www.oecd.org/document/16/ 0,3343,en_2649_33929_2085200_1_1_1_1,00.html, referenced March 17, 2010.

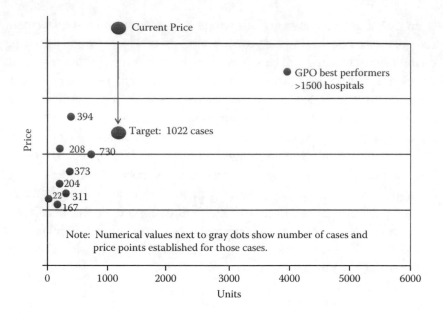

FIGURE 3.4
Market pricing for total knee replacement.

a new decision-making process that was stakeholder-centric and that led to greater collaboration among physicians, clinicians, administrators, and suppliers. The hospital system also broadened its medical director of supply chain position, which was filled by a practicing surgeon. This individual would become the voice of the physician community in all supply chain decisions.

Next, the CSO adopted a category management approach, as is commonly used in other industries, to examine the total spend of the hospital system, and discovered that in some cases spending was not being effectively tracked and measured. Further, it was found that comparatively little analysis had been done around certain major supply categories, and further, that many physicians had never even been involved in previous sourcing decisions. Although many activities were occurring during this period, one of the most important components of change was to focus on *category teams* that were led by a supply management executive, but engaged multiple clinical and financial stakeholders in these decisions and focused on a clear and compelling *category strategy*. Sourcing leaders facilitated the meetings, did much of the data collection and analysis, but decisions were to be made on a consensus basis, with input taken from all of the stakeholders.

The category of operations studied initially was total joint replacement. More than 193,000 total hip replacements and 581,000 total knee replacements are performed each year in the United States. Similar surgical procedures are performed on other joints, including the shoulder and elbow.* This is an important area of medical care, because in the United States musculoskeletal conditions cost society up to $254 billion per year in medical care and lost productivity. Musculoskeletal conditions are the number one reason that patients visit doctors. A hip or knee replacement costs an average of about $45,000,† Not surprisingly, replacement costs in the United States are the highest in the world, with Thailand, Singapore, and other regions performing similar surgeries at half the cost.

As hospital operations begins to identify opportunities for risk mitigation and total cost improvement in areas such as total joint replacement, total cost should include not just the price of the product or implant, but more importantly the total costs of operating on the patient, their subsequent hospital stay, and any potential additional costs that are borne by either the hospital or the patient. To do so, hospitals need to quickly identify the need to include physicians as stakeholders. There are often barriers within operations that inhibit the advance to engage physician stakeholders, and even if begun, they are generally unsuccessful in engaging physicians and reaching agreement. The source of this frustration is elevated and often noted in discussions, with finger-pointing and accusatory claims based on the physician working environment, patient care limitations, and historic issues rather than operations' current interests. This continued state fuels a culture that is not only counter-productive for the hospital, but also for the physician and for patient outcomes.

One of the first category teams established was in an area that had a high degree of clinical sensitivity and value: hip and knee joint replacements. Because this was the first major category project undertaken by the new supply chain team, it was decided to proceed in a two-phased approach. Phase 1 would entail engaging physicians to review spend analytics around this family of purchases, and establish goals for *market price competitiveness* based on current market analysis across the United States and usage across the entire IDN. Phase 2 would then take a deeper dive into understanding the true cost drivers behind the two procedures of hip and knee

---

* American Association of Orthopedic Surgeons, "Total Hip Replacement," http://orthoinfo.aaos. org/topic.cfm?topic=A00377, accessed March 15, 2010.
† That Must Be Bob. I Hear His New Hip Squeaking. *New York Times,* May 11, 2008 http://www. nytimes.com/2008/05/11/business/11hip.html?_r=0

replacement, and begin to establish criteria for what types of replacement items should optimally be utilized based on physician recommendations and economics. This in essence would be a surgeon- and supplier-derived demand matching process as well as an operations initiative to improve OR and inpatient efficiencies. It is important to note that Phase 1 was a key element to success, for without an early *win*, physicians and operations would likely lose interest and thus be less likely to participate in Phase 2.

The CSO selected physicians that were the "power users"—surgeons who performed the most hip and knee procedures—to be part of the team. These physicians were not selected based on their reputation as easy-going collaborators; rather, they were a true representation of the majority of users at different locations that consumed the bulk of these products in their daily surgeries. In order to complete the collaborative model, senior hospital operations executives participated on the team, along with their respective surgeons.

At the first Phase 2 team meeting, the data on current state of joint replacements were presented and explained (Figure 3.4). With over 1,700 replacements a year, this IDN was experiencing service-line revenue losses within this category, due to the fact that each of its hospitals was negotiating independently with seven different suppliers. They next introduced a draft team charter that established team objectives, the governance structure, roles and responsibilities of team members, and deliverables from the team. They also introduced a compelling figure that illustrated the IDN current pricing structure relative to other hospitals (Figure 3.5). Based on the current pricing profile, the organization was paying significantly more than lower-volume hospitals were for both knee and hip (not shown) implants. In most cases, this was due to higher price agreements. When the team viewed this data, there was universal consensus from the surgeons that this was a problem that needed to be resolved and was clearly an unsustainable situation. The team agreed that the objective in this case was to "Achieve near average market pricing for implants … to influence and champion the agreed upon Total Joint Hip and Knee Supply Strategy, including strategy execution across all Ministry hospitals." The team established a savings threshold for both hip and knee replacement implants and determined the supplier's flexibility to meet that threshold. This target was determined based on mid-market pricing research as shown in Figure 3.4. The team agreed with the surgeons in a consensus manner concerning what that savings thresholds should be given the market research. The first meeting concluded by noting, "There are only two entities in the world

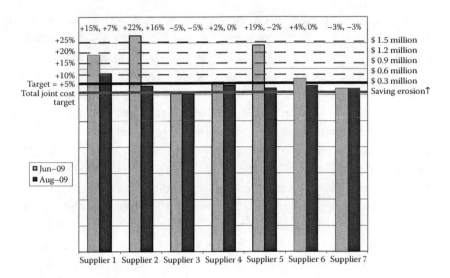

FIGURE 3.5
Hip and knee joint cost savings targets.

who know the product or service better than anyone else ... and that is the people that make it (suppliers) and the people that use it (physicians/ clinicians). If we don't better engage both these groups, we won't have to worry about 'total cost' management of procedures such as hip and knee replacement because it cannot happen without this critical input."

At the next team meeting in June 2009, an additional set of compelling data was brought to the table (see Figure 3.5). Based on current contracted pricing agreements, it was discovered that *all* of the seven suppliers currently providing joints to were well above the targeted price (see left bar for each supplier). In fact, only a few of the seven had agreed to do something about their pricing structure. Based on this data, the team was offered three options: (a) do nothing, and live with the current pricing structure, (b) put some effort into this to extract some smaller price reductions and yet keep all seven suppliers, or (c) have a deeper conversation with suppliers on the value of the relationship that the team was seeking to establish with them in the future with a more meaningful savings threshold for the implants used. The risk with the latter option was that the team might not like the outcome, and that it could negatively impact other surgeons' views on this approach. Going around the table, the physicians and operations executive agreed by unanimous consensus that Option 3 was the appropriate approach.

When the second round of deeper conversations was completed with suppliers, the results were again compiled and shown to the team.

The decision was then questioned further: Should we raise our target (Figure 3.5) by 10% or 20%? Because if the division was to raise the bar, this would make it easier for suppliers to come into the competitive range, and hence produce less of a need to change suppliers, but it had the drawback of also lessening the cost savings aligned with market pricing, which was a key deliverable. This question was raised at the next meeting and the physicians and operations team came back with their own decision: they felt that the original target should be raised, but only very minimally. This decision was *not* made by the sourcing executive—it was explicitly made by physicians and operations. This is the power of the collaboration model at work.

The team then decided on an outcome. The suppliers who agreed to the pricing benchmark would be named tier 1 contract suppliers. By definition, a tier 1 supplier has met all of the IDN's pricing requirements, meaning that any surgeon in the system is approved to use them in their procedures and the suppliers were allowed to keep inventory on-site at the hospitals. However, a tier 2 contract supplier could be utilized solely for emergency revisions, or *second-sided* surgery in patients who already had the same product on the other side, but their inventory would not be kept on-site. The physician/operations/supply chain team also established that tier 2 suppliers could, at any time, become a tier 1 preferred supplier if they met the required savings threshold. Shortly thereafter, some tier 2 suppliers asked if they could be admitted to tier 1 status. This is but one example of the *influence model* versus the command-and-control model. Additionally, this is an example of the "and" model (e.g., no significant change in suppliers/products and no compliance and volume level needed to achieve cost savings) versus the "or" model (e.g., the only way to get cost savings is to limit suppliers and drive volume and compliance). This key learning, that an "and" model does indeed work in healthcare, which is fundamental in just about every other industry, was an "Aha" moment for many.

In the next stage, Phase 2, all suppliers were invited to engage more closely with the physician and operations community to identify optimal strategies for improving patient outcomes, further reducing unnecessary costs via streamlining and simplifying processes, identifying appropriate joints for different types of patients (known as demand management), and ongoing collaborative discussions. This initiative is currently moving forward with significant engagement from physicians, operations, and suppliers to develop a total cost approach that considers which total joints are best for which types of patients as well as improving operations.

4

Supply Chain Network Analytics for the Healthcare Industry Assessing Best of Breed

INTRODUCTION

Healthcare providers are facing continued lower operating margins, increased risks, and potentially once-in-a-lifetime healthcare reform. With this backdrop, there is an increasing focus on supply chain management as a means to minimize risk, optimize operating costs, improve revenue, improve operating margin, and hence enable the hospital to better serve the patient. Executives are now recognizing that health providers have relatively immature supply chains, and that development of strategic management of supply chains is generally at a nascent level.[*] Healthcare organizations typically proceed through an evolution of basic processes in supply management.[†] Initially, many providers are not focused on managing the supply chain, but rely on an external group purchasing organization to negotiate all of their contracts, and focus on driving compliance in the physician community. Organizations seeking to drive change must begin by establishing a charter to do so with their executive team, and make a commitment to moving away from a transaction price–based focus. Another critical element at this stage of development is the ability to isolate and measure *where* and *how* third-party spending is occurring in healthcare systems, through improved spend management.

---

[*] E. Schneller and L. R. Smeltzer. *Strategic Management of the Health Care Supply Chain* (San Francisco: John Wiley, 2006).
[†] Ibid.

The healthcare industry is in the early stages of deploying spend analytics solutions, and executives are faced with many challenges in this regard. As we approach a new era in the healthcare industry with increasing network complexity and stringent budgets, the need to better control costs is a direct function of healthcare management's ability to isolate, track, and manage third-party spending.[*]

According to Gendron and D'Onofrio,[†] improving the integrity of spend across a complex value chain of the healthcare industry is a fundamental element in building a strong foundation for supply management.

Although these facts are widely recognized by executives, the spend management landscape is not well defined in healthcare. Many different database and procurement systems exist. The development of standardized item masters, coding structures, and nomenclatures are in a nascent form. Finally, multiple providers of spend management technologies are claiming to offer the best solutions, ranging from software providers, group purchasing organizations (GPOs), and third-party providers. In an effort to better assess this landscape and identify appropriate governance structures, technology requirements, industry trends, and contracting guidelines, the NC State University Supply Chain Resource Cooperative (http://scm.ncsu.edu) engaged industry leaders and subject matter experts in an industry assessment of spend management healthcare solutions. The methodology used to carry out this study is described next.

METHODOLOGY

Why is it important to capture supply chain spending transaction-level data associated with third-party purchasing processes? Because from time to time the healthcare supply chain system must identify opportunities for savings through a process known as a *spend analysis*. A spend analysis becomes a critical input into building category strategies, but spend management involves the ongoing maintenance, update, and refinement of the spend data to make it useful for decision making.

---

[*] Jason Byrnes, "Fixing the Healthcare Supply Chain," Harvard Business School, April 5, 2004, http://hbswk.hbs.edu/archive/4036.html, accessed June 27, 2010.

[†] M. S. Gendron and M. J. D'Onofrio, "Data Quality in the Healthcare Industry," *Data Quality* 7, no. 1 (2001).

Category strategy development is a process applied to general families of purchased products or services that seek to optimize spending while meeting or exceeding stakeholder requirements. (Stakeholders may include physicians, clinical and nonclinical staff, and administrators, facilities management, etc.)

A spend analysis was often viewed as a one-time annual event to derive budgeting estimates and develop insights into annual contract negotiations. Today, spend analysis is evolving into spend management, which is a much more dynamic and ongoing assessment and tracking of spending patterns, matched to other cost drivers and activities. Spend analysis does not need to occur only on an annual basis, but can also be applied to reviews of a category or subcategory of spend that occurs when a contract is being negotiated, or when a strategic sourcing project is initiated for a particular category group. Spend analysis is also a critical component of effective budget planning, and setting key performance indicators for sourcing teams to consider in their assigned duties. An ongoing spend management capability provides answers to the following questions:

- What did the provider spend its money on over the past year? This value is an important component in calculating the cost of goods sold in the financial statement. Purchased goods and materials are often more than 40% of the total cost of goods sold in healthcare. Many systems fail to include indirect and nonclinical spending in their analysis, which is missing an important piece of the pie.
- Did the healthcare system receive the contracted level of products and services based on payments made to third parties? Although many providers outsource their purchasing to GPOs, there is nevertheless a need to audit and verify that services and products delivered met not only contracted pricing, but also service level agreements, statements of work, and appropriate levels of support services. A thorough spend analysis will often reveal areas where products and services are being paid for, but the goods or services are not even being received or being used by the system.
- Which suppliers received the majority of the business, and did they charge an accurate price across all the units in comparison to the requirements in the purchase orders (POs, contracts, and statements of work?) This is an important component to ensure contract compliance.

- Which divisions of the business spent their money on products and services that were correctly budgeted for? (This is an important component for planning annual budgets for spending in the coming year.)
- Are there opportunities to combine volumes of spending from different parts of the healthcare system, and standardize product requirements, reduce the number of suppliers providing these products, or exploit market conditions to receive better pricing? (This is an important input into strategic sourcing).

Moreover, spend management provides insights and clarity into these questions and yields an important planning document for senior executives in healthcare operations, supply management, and finance. Despite the importance of this capability, many healthcare systems struggle to develop a comprehensive and accurate spend analysis report. This is because purchasing was for many years a paper-based system, and figures were not entered correctly into accounting systems. Even with the evolution of sophisticated enterprise systems such as SAP and Oracle, purchasing transactions are often entered incorrectly, which brings to mind the old phrase "garbage in, garbage out." Another problem is that many enterprises have grown through mergers and acquisitions. When a new division is acquired, it may be using a different system from the acquiring system, and so the data is not easily translatable. For this reason, many healthcare systems are undergoing major initiatives to streamline procurement through electronic procurement systems that will revamp the purchase-to-pay process and automate different portions to capture transactions more effectively. Indeed, research suggests that best-in-class firms are more likely to have a higher proportion of their spend under management, which has led to important improvements such as cost reductions, reduction of noncompliant purchases, supply base reduction, and electronically enabled suppliers.

Assessing the Spend Management Landscape

A research team was assembled that performed a thorough analysis of spend analysis best practices. A number of industry subject matter experts were consulted, including academics, spend management industry experts, healthcare consultants, and healthcare executives. Based on these views, a taxonomy of capabilities was developed around the core elements of a spend management program, which include the following:

- Data cleansing (acquisition, cleansing, preparation, and database population)
- Spend analytics
- Contract management
- Technology management
- Customer service

A capability assessment was defined for each category based on user input that provided guidelines for assessing the level of maturity (basic, typical, or advanced) of different providers in each of these five areas, with a scoring mechanism determined. This scorecard was used as the basis for assessing the capabilities of each provider.

The spend management landscape includes a number of different providers of spend management services. It quickly became apparent that a significant variance in capabilities claimed in marketing materials did not always align with demonstrated experience of these same providers, and is shown in the Appendix within this chapter.

The population of firms sampled for this study included the following:

- **Group purchasing organizations (4):** Labeled as GPO1, GPO2, GPO3, and GPO4. These providers covered some but not all of the capabilities in the study.
- **Distributors (4):** Labeled as D1, D2, D3, and D4. Two of these distributors did not provide significant spend management capabilities, but for the most part outsourced capabilities to a third party.
- **Specialized software providers (4):** Labeled as SS1, SS2, SS3, and SS4. These are companies that focused on different spend management capabilities, including data acquisition, cleansing, preparation, and database upload. They also provided different forms of services for contract management, spend analytics, technology, and customer service. These firms were either operating as software-as-a-service providers or providers with specialized assets.
- **Other software providers (3):** These organizations provide benchmarking and database support that allows providers to compare their current pricing and spend patterns to other healthcare companies. They possessed limited capabilities in data cleansing.

- **Enterprise resource planning (ERP) providers (2):** These organizations supported large ERP platforms used in healthcare and provided varying levels of support around spend management.

All of these organizations claim to provide spend management support services in one form or another. Because of the diversity of the actual services provided, there was a need for a rigorous scoring system that would provide a means to identify each firm's true capabilities.

Identifying capabilities was not as easy as it might sound. Moreover, while many providers had marketing materials or generic demonstrations on their websites alleging certain capabilities in data cleansing, spend analysis, contract management, and services, further research by our team revealed that these capabilities could not be effectively validated. Validation of capabilities was performed through several means. First, we conducted interviews with healthcare executives, software providers, and subject matter experts familiar with provider capabilities. Second, we reviewed recent studies conducted by the U.S. Department of Defense (DoD) on data quality in the industry, and reviewed other publications and industry presentations at recent healthcare supply chain conferences that we attended. Finally, we contacted each of the providers and emphasized to them that this study was forthcoming, and that we would welcome the opportunity to review their stated capabilities through client references, demonstrations, or other mechanisms. Unfortunately, our repeated requests for interviews often went unanswered, suggesting that these providers were indeed reluctant to provide validation of their spend management solutions. It also became apparent through the validation process that many of the capabilities alleged in marketing materials did not meet even the *basic* level of performance identified in our scoring mechanism. In fact, it was not even apparent that a single customer existed who had successfully implemented some of these services! As such, we provided a lower score to providers that refused an interview or where we were unable to ascertain actual capabilities based on a demonstration or client references or testimonials.

In the following sections, we assess each vendor's capabilities along each of the five dimensions, and provide a summary score using the following scorecard.

Defining Components of Supply Chain Spend Analytics

Understanding the components of spend analytics management was an important first task before assessing the landscape of different solutions. Jason Busch, widely recognized as the leading expert on spend management based on his blog SpendMatters.com, wrote in a recent article about the roots of spend management technology.* He noted that the initial goals of spend analysis software were to build a toolset that would include the following capabilities:

- The ability to collect and analyze data across multiple operating units, systems, instances, and versions, including but not limited to ERP (e.g., accounts payable [A/P] data)
- Advanced data cleansing and analysis
- Common commodity classification and structure (e.g., United Nations Standard Products and Services Code [UNSPSC])
- Item-level visibility (especially in the case of direct materials)
- The need to build repeatability and sustainability into a process versus taking on spend analysis as a one-time effort

Busch also notes that initial efforts by his firm, FreeMarkets, in the 1990s essentially amounted to a largely manual extract, transform, load (ETL) data management process that loaded information into a relational database, on top of which sat a Cognos platform (i.e., business intelligence) with a number of canned reports. The FreeMarkets approach, like many others at the time, was not elegant, but it worked in helping answer a number of basic questions that could be used in a cost reduction strategy.

Some of the basic questions that spend visibility can answer for a buying organization included:

1. What is my total spend?
2. Who are my largest suppliers (parts, spend, categories)?
3. What are my largest spend segments?
4. Which parts are growing in total spend? Shrinking?
5. Which parts have the largest price inflation (over a given period of time)?
6. Am I paying more to one supplier than another for part X?
7. Where can I quickly cut costs by taking action?

---

* Jason Busch, "Beyond the Basics: Using Spend Visibility to Drive More Than Category Sourcing Strategies and Spend Reporting," *Spend Matters* Compass Series, 2010, Volume 2.

Other more advanced questions that spend visibility tools could answer included the following areas:

1. Contract Management
   a. Am I paying the contract price?
   b. How much am I buying off contract?
   c. Why? (e.g., noncompliance, expediting, etc.)
2. Buyer Management
   a. Who is managing the most items/spend?
   b. Who is managing this contract?
3. Spend Disbursement
   a. Percent of spend from low-cost countries?
   b. Percent of spend from Minority Women-Owned Enterprises (MWE)?
4. Time Variance
   a. What has changed over the past year?
   b. Why has the variance occurred (e.g., restocking vs. demand-driven replenishment based on a pull model)?
5. Management, Leverage, and Planning
   a. Who should own commodity X?
   b. How can we best leverage similar items (but potentially with different stock keeping unit [SKU]/part numbers and suppliers) across operating unit?

For purposes of this report, *supply chain analytics* is defined by five distinct processes that span software systems, process management, and decision support, as shown in Figure 4.1: (1) data cleansing (which includes data acquisition, cleansing, preparation, and database population), (2) spend analytics, (3) contract management, (4) technology applications, and (5) customer service. While we acknowledge that different providers have varying perceptions of the different forms of spend data management approaches, we have selected these categories based on common best practices not just in healthcare, but other industries as well. The report assesses current solutions in the marketplace based on these five core processes. These categories were selected based on the factors that were identified with healthcare and data solutions providers as being the most critical in selecting spend management solutions. Other factors that were *not considered* in this report include the spend management vendor's prior experience in providing solutions, customer credibility,

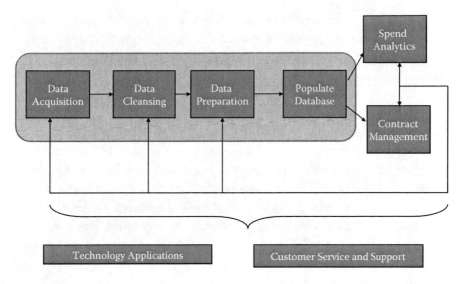

FIGURE 4.1
Core supply chain analytics processes.

and alignment with customer requirements. These elements were deemed specific to a given healthcare provider's situation and context.

Next, we describe each of the elements shown in Figure 4.1, define the components of each element, and provide the scoring mechanism. The assessment score for each provider reviewed in this study is provided, and observations and key trends are discussed.

Data Cleansing

Access to the right data is essential, as accurate and properly coded data provide the foundation for category management strategies, including leveraging, pricing agreements, quantity discounts, value analysis, supply base optimization, and other important cost management activities. Data cleansing is actually a process that involves four stages, as shown in Figure 4.1.

Data Acquisition

First, the user is contacted and the raw data are collected from different sources. Common sources of data can be the customer's Materials Management Information System (MMIS), GPO, and local suppliers. It is important at this stage that *all* relevant spend data, including indirect spend, are included in the analysis. Note that many providers restrict their data acquisition to only electronic data interchange (EDI) data, or inventory data that is readily available, thereby missing a significant chunk of the total spend. The net impact of this oversight is that it provides an inaccurate representation of what the healthcare system is truly spending on third-party goods and services.

Data Cleansing

Busch notes that from a technical perspective, first generation-spend analysis approaches were limited by the underlying architecture, development, and the analytical and visualization capabilities available to providers at the time. This is still a major problem for healthcare providers. The limits of relational database technology based on disk storage and traditional data warehousing approaches to storing, querying, and accessing information and reports are one example of the constraints that are often encountered, due to old technology platforms. A few healthcare systems are now beginning to invest in the usage of in-memory databases that rely on main memory (or RAM, as it's better known) storage approaches that can materially increase query speeds as well as workarounds to traditional storage and query models that greatly increase both the speed with which we can search and access information as well as the ability to search information sets in the context of each other.[*]

One of the most important challenges in healthcare is that the data coming from manufacturers and suppliers of healthcare supplies are flawed even before they reach the hospital's analytics team. A recent study by the Department of Defense[†] conducted significant analyses of item data collected from various DoD suppliers and found significant data disconnects between healthcare industry trading partners. This poor connectivity included poor data accuracy among manufacturers, distributors, and the DoD's own internal pricing and contract management applications. Further, the study found that the process of requesting "one-off" data feeds from partners was a significant resource burden on all parties involved. As shown in Figure 4.2, up to 20% of manufacturer data has errors that are transmitted to distributors and other third parties, with further data errors occurring in other parts of the channel as well. This means that much of the data that are already assumed to be "clean" that are imported into databases for spend analysis are already rife with error.

---

[*] Busch, Jason. "Beyond the Basics."
[†] *Creating a Source of Truth in Healthcare: Testing the GDSN as a Platform for the Healthcare Product Data Utility Results from DoD Healthcare GDSN Pilot Phase IIA*, U.S. Department of Defense/Veteran's Administration Data Synchronization Study, September 2007.

	Manufacturer	Distributor	GPO	Customer
Missing Middle Levels of Packaging	15–20%	1–4%	20–25%	15–25%
Hard "Packaging Quantity" Errors	1%	1%	2%	2–5%
Unit of Measure Confusion/Misuse	2–6%	1–3%	2–5%	Unknown
Missing Packaging–not Middle Level	3–8%	3–8%	3–7%	5%
Manufacturer Name Problems	NA	2–5%	1–4%	30%
Obsolete Products	1–4%	2–5%	1–8%	5–15%
Missing Product Brand Names	2–5%	5–10%	5–10%	20–25%
Incomplete Item Descriptions	5–15%	3–12%	5–15%	10–20%
Wrong Customer Unit Prices	Unknown	1–2%	NA	1–2%
Customer Paid More than Lowest Contract Price	NA	Unknown	NA	3–6%

FIGURE 4.2
The DoD Data Synchronization Study quantified industry-wide data problems.

Data Classification and Preparation

One of the most important foundational shifts in spend analysis technology in the past eighteen months has been an interest in greater flexibility and visibility into the classification process. Increasingly, more advanced organizations are starting to look for the ability to classify spend to one or more taxonomies at the same time (e.g., customized UNSPSC and ERP materials code) as well as having the ability to reclassify spend to analyze different views and cuts of the data based on functional roles and objectives. Moreover, some organizations are looking to exert greater control over the spend visibility process; these individuals are often becoming distrustful of "black box" approaches to gathering and analyzing spend data. Coding of data is essential when conducting category analyses and clinical effectiveness studies. For example, a hospital wanting to gain strategic advantage through public reporting on clinical excellence will require an understanding of the impact of products on reducing hospital-acquired infections and contributing to the total episode of care and a preference for "smart products."* An example is pumps that provide feedback on the accuracy of dosage delivery. Category analysis using data classification codes can also identify areas where *system internal cosourcing* is taking place. This refers to situations involving decisions

---

* Eugene Schneller, "A Guide to Successful Strategic Sourcing," *Materials Management in Healthcare* 19, no. 6 (2010): 22–25.

regarding commodity items as well as physician preference items and the actual determination of vendors, where there continues to be a duplication of purchasing efforts at both hospital and system levels. This is an expensive proposition that includes duplication of effort for identifying products and suppliers, developing and managing requests for proposal and information, optimizing proposals, and obtaining offers, finalizing awards, and implementing and monitoring contracts. As systems migrate from being holding companies to operating companies, reduction of internal cosourcing is an important strategic opportunity, but will rely on effective data cleansing and coding as the basis for analysis and action.

It is important to note here that some providers we spoke with believed that data cleansing is not as valuable as data normalization. The point was made that normalization does not have to clean the data to make effective use of the resulting analysis. We disagree with this point for several reasons. First, if data normalization was acceptable without cleansing, healthcare would not be adopting GS1 standards to address the issue of manufacturers publishing data with a "warranty" of accuracy. Accurate and clean data are critical for any type of analytics or normalization effort. In this case, if "garbage" goes in, then the resulting output is more likely to be "garbage" as well.

Database Population

Finally, the coded dataset is uploaded into the requisite application. Once uploaded, the real power of the data can be leveraged through merging with other data forms for benchmarking and cross-reference analyses. Application and data integration paradigms have already shifted in a number of nonhealthcare applications from one of batch uploads from multiple source systems to real-time data queries that can search hundreds (or more) disparate sources while normalizing, classifying, and cleansing information at the point of query. In the coming years, Oracle, IBM, and D&B, all of which have purchased customer data integration (CDI) vendors, could begin to apply these techniques to spend and supplier information as well. Incidentally, Oracle is the first to market in the procurement space with a supply-focused product that leverages CDI technology (gained from its Siebel acquisition), although at the time of publication, this technology is not currently available from a procurement use case perspective. CDI technology actually improves the integrity of the data from individual sources, allowing users to match and link disparate information sources with varying levels of accuracy. CDI tools can correct for data-entry mistakes, such as misspellings, across different data sources to provide an accurate picture. Here again, the ability to accurately match UNSPSC codes to items is dependent on the accuracy and transparency of the original dataset.

One of the important questions to note in this four-stage process is, "Who owns the cleansed and coded data?" It is important to note that not all providers will share the results of a cleansing activity with the customer. In some cases, they may elect to clean it only as input into their particular application (e.g., contracting, GPO services, etc.). Without direct access and ownership of the cleansed dataset, performing in-depth category analysis is not possible, which is the equivalent of restricting internal access to one's own books! Trusting that a GPO or third party will conduct their due diligence and perform spend analyses on your behalf is a naïve assumption that merits further consideration.

Some of the providers we reviewed had systems that should recognize a product and enrich it with the correct manufacturer name and item number, UNSPSC code, and descriptions, before uploading it into an ERP application. However, these providers acknowledged that not every product code was matched, leaving an unknown number of items with no match that were not uploaded into the contract database. Here again, the importance of cleansed data is critical.

An automated process augmented with a manual process is the current standard in the healthcare industry that increases efficiency and accuracy. Customer service is important in this stage, because involving personnel with the expertise, such as clinicians, to manage data is one of the key checkpoints for customers in choosing vendors. Proper coding of the data will require engaging clinical experts, as well as other functional groups such as facilities, logistics, IT, legal, marketing, and finance, to truly make sense of the data. This is critical to arrive at strategic sourcing decisions that will be effective. In this regard, a third party should be willing to provide a level of consulting and coordination that is consistent with the level of effort required to perform a thorough spend management project.

As shown in Table 4.1, data cleansing was assessed across four major categories.

1. What is the vendor's capability for acquiring data in multiple formats from multiple sources in building the master data file?
2. What is the ability of the vendor to verify and normalize data, and to capture all existing data including unmatched data?

TABLE 4.1

Data Cleansing Assessment Score

	Basic	Typical	Advanced
Item master build (7)	Accepts current item master file as is.	Collects MMIS purchase order and item master file; analyzes by spend and delivers result to hospital.	Collects core files from all supply chain departments, analyzes by spend, and consults with hospital on final item master file.
Verification of distributor catalog number, manufacturer, manufacturer catalog number, catalog description, and packaging data (7)	Data is normalized in its current state without reference to an existing database.	Matches precleansed data to an existing database. Unmatched has no action taken. Packaging accepted at purchase UOM.	Matches precleansed data to an existing database. Unmatched manually verified at product source. Packaging researched to low UOM.
Description standardization (6)	Reorganization of current client description to follow vendor-decided naming convention.	Rules and abbreviations are provided by vendor with standard schema for use with every client.	Rules and abbreviations are customizable per client needs. Vendor has clinicians write descriptions.
Item classification (5)	Applies a proprietary classification schema not based on an external standard.	Applies UNSPSC codes to items.	Applies UNSPSC codes to items and provides clinical equivalency.

3. What is the ability of the vendor to create item descriptions that meet the client's needs and what is the breadth of this capability?
4. Does the vendor provide a universal item classification scheme (e.g., UNSPSC) to allow data to be classified into industry standards and provide clinical equivalency?

The results of the assessment of data cleansing capabilities are shown in Figure 4.3.

As shown in the chart, there are only really two specialized software firms and one distributor that provide the capability to perform a thorough

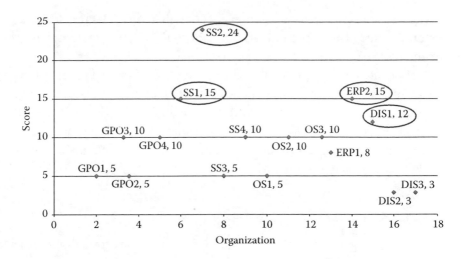

FIGURE 4.3
Data cleansing (max score = 25).

data-cleansing process. There are several reasons for this result. (Note that the ERP provider, ERP2, uses SS1 as its data cleansing platform). First, as noted earlier, there is a fundamental problem with most providers who assume that data integrity coming from suppliers is acceptable, when in fact the DoD study clearly indicated that the data are, in most cases, not only highly suspect, but highly inaccurate. Up to 20% of manufacturer data were shown to contain errors. Most providers do not take the time or the due diligence to improve the integrity of these data before they are entered into proprietary databases. In reality, SS1 and DIS1 are assuming that data coming from the manufacturer are not tainted, which results in a lower score. Second, a key cleansing component is categorization. As noted in the assessment scale, classification and coding of the data using UNSPSC or other standard code can only be associated with data that are completely clean. Third, many of the parties in this study do not perform their own data cleansing process, but outsource it to third parties in India or specialized domestic data cleansing providers (such as SS2, who was interviewed for this study.) Fourth, many of the providers do not cleanse the data and then provide them back to the client. Instead, they cleanse data solely for purposes of entering them into their database and contracts portfolio or spend analytics tool.

Only SS1 and SS2 use an automated front end to a catalog and are selling an actual data cleansing and classification service, which can be turned over to the actual client *or* entered into their own catalog service tool. In particular, GPOs and ERP providers cleanse the data only if there is an exclusiveity agreement to use their proprietary database system. In such cases, the upload may not touch every line item, which means less than 70% of the spend data may be included. In this case, not all of the data have UNSPSC coding, and no standard descriptions are assigned for much of the spend data. For distributors, significant discrepancies between actual item codes and database codes are believed to exist. Finally, multiple vendors refused to provide a demo or further information, leaving us to believe that many of the claims in their marketing material are invalid.

Contract Management

Contract management systems provide visibility into historical purchase order and contract data for an integrated delivery network (IDN) or hospital. A good contract management tool typically stores various types of contracts such as GPO and local manufacturers. The system should allow a sourcing team to easily search and edit the contract catalog. Some vendors provide access to their catalogs, which can help customers to broaden their supplier base. Customers also look for real-time updates on contract data and purchase data, at the same time taking advantage of additional contract opportunities. All this information should typically be easily accessible via dashboards and reports that provide easy comprehension of data. Contract visibility improves compliance and can promote contract utilization and help to reduce maverick spend.

The criteria for assessing contract management capabilities is shown in Table 4.2.

1. Are physical contracts available in the application? Can they be classified in a searchable archive that permits search and reporting capabilities?
2. Will the contract management system handle multiple forms of contracts, including GPO, local, and nonsupply contracts?
3. What is the reporting capability of the system? Does it allow robust reporting of all supply contracts by type, buyer, date, and other criteria?
4. What are the search capabilities of the system? Is the data warehouse searchable using item-level detail, original equipment manufacturer (OEM) or distributor information across both local and GPO contracts?

TABLE 4.2

Contract Management Assessment

	Basic	Typical	Advanced
Physical copies of contracts are available in application	Contracts are in a searchable archive with limited vendor predefined search criteria	Contracts are in a searchable archive with multiple vendor predefined search criteria	Contracts are in a searchable archive with multiple vendor predefined search criteria as well as custom hospital-specific criteria (e.g., department and buyer codes)
Contract types handled	GPO only	GPO contracts, but locals manually uploaded by hospital with limited access	Contract warehouse holds any type of contract (e.g., GPO, local, and nonsupply)
Reporting capability	User can obtain reports on a single group of GPO contracts	Reporting available by contract class, type, and OEM on GPO contracts only	Robust reporting of all supply contracts by type, buyer, date, OEM, class, tiers, rebates, renewal, etc.
Item-level detail	Items are tied to contracts. Search is limited to contract header or contract name for GPO contracts only	Items are tied to contracts. Search is limited to contract header or contract name for GPO and local contracts	Contract warehouse is searchable by item-level detail using OEM or distributor information and reports across all contracts, local and GPO

Several characteristics of contract management providers suggest that there exists significant variance in demonstrated capabilities, as shown in Figure 4.4. First, because much of the original spend data is not included in spend databases, matching contractual terms against purchase orders and invoices provides a challenge in most of the systems assessed in this study. Second, there are problems that exist from a conflict-of-interest perspective with utilizing GPO contract databases. Because a GPO has a vested interest to ensure that an IDN or hospital uses their sources of supply exclusively, many of these systems prevent the customer from conducting an independent spend analysis that could provide alternative outcomes. For example, if the output of a spend analysis reveals that a customer should move away

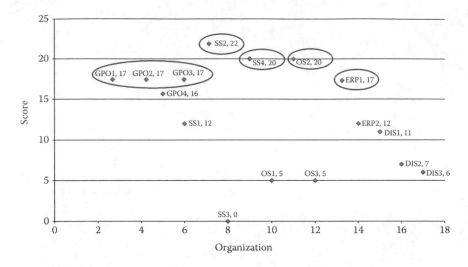

FIGURE 4.4
Contract management (max score = 25).

from a GPO portfolio and use a local contract, the GPO would lose revenue. To prevent this from occurring, visibility into spend data may be purposefully limited by GPOs.

A third issue discovered in the analysis is that even specialized software providers only allow organizations to connect to their servers via an EDI connection, which acts as a central repository to manage orders and contracts electronically. Non-EDI data is not included in contracted spend, which prevents full leveraging of an IDN's spend, due to the fact that a large portion of the item file/contracts is not included. In some cases, organizations have limited contracting capabilities and were rated a zero. In the case of ERP providers, much of the data is not included if it is in a nondigital format, or is outsourced to a third party. Customers also expressed frustration in using ERP contract modules, which do not always include paper contracts. Finally, demonstrations of actual capabilities were mostly unavailable.

Of the specialized software providers, only SS2 actually worked with clients to include all relevant contract data. All of the GPOs were rated lower due to the aforementioned rationale and lack of capability, while one of the ERP providers had a reasonably well-run contract management system, which however did not include all contract data. Also noteworthy was a specialized healthcare contracting company (OS2), which has a well-developed online real-time customized centralized contract database focused on healthcare. SS4 is another company with an advanced contract management tool that utilizes a web-based application that makes it cheap and user friendly. A number of providers in our study use their contract and analysis software tool for contract management and the bidding process. Once again, however, these providers use a data normalization process without an upront data cleansing effort, which means that contract data quality is not validated as accurate.

Spend Analytics

As noted in the introduction to this chapter, controlling costs and establishing a structure for analyzing costs has become a critical issue for healthcare providers. Organizations' spending often exceeds projected spending due to discrepancies and disparities that prevail within the data resource. One of the biggest challenges that exist is the silos of data in most healthcare organizations. ERP transactional data mitigates this challenge when multitier visibility to data is combined with the application of industry standard taxonomies that allow proper grouping of data into "buckets" often called *categories*. When a category of spend is defined, (e.g., IT spend, facilities, transportation, etc.), it can be broken down further into subcategories (e.g., hardware, software, consulting, etc.), which permits the application of a strategic sourcing process (also called *category management strategy development*). The ability to create this information, enforce a taxonomy standard, and apply analysis at the back end of the sourcing process, is of paramount importance. Only then can direct and indirect spending be measured, renegotiated, benchmarked, throttled (e.g., by reducing demand), and ultimately controlled.[*] Acquiring this capability is not simply a matter of having the right software. Spend management is, in effect, a learning mechanism for healthcare organizations. It requires not just the software, but the combination of technology, consulting, and engagement of subject matter experts to define and create the operational structure for measuring and assessing third-party spend. There is no single "magic bullet" that takes care of this problem. Each organization is unique, with its own set of users and requirements. In most cases, healthcare providers themselves are not aware of their needs and requirements! But our general experience in carrying out this study is that they desire to have a single-package tool that can take care of all of their issues. As we explored

---

[*] R. B. Handfield, *Supply Market Intelligence* (Boca Raton, FL: Auerbach, 2008).

our data, we learned that single-package tools are not available at this time. All of the providers have different specialties and functional elements. So ultimately, there is a trade-off that healthcare providers must make in selecting a spend management service provider.

The fundamental objective of a spend analysis is to collect historical data by commodity, relative to demand from the lines of business, with the exception of personnel expenses, occupancy, and corporate spend. The data should go into the appropriate level of unit-level detail required for analysis and category management, and should also be rolled up at an aggregate level on every element of what is spent. The result is a common understanding of historical spending relative to demand from each end user within an organization, based on accurate information collected through defined and automated procure-to-pay systems. Spend analysis requires that you drive all spend to a unit of consumption and a rate of consumption. The output of spend analysis is used to drive demand management, commodity management, and risk management strategies. It is fundamental to communicate to the business partners to ensure understanding of where they spent their money and why it was spent.[*]

Busch also emphasizes the power of spend analytics when combined with other forms of data. He notes:[†]

> Consider the current batch-based limitations and challenges of current systems, including spend visibility tools, supplier performance management systems, and supplier information management. These tools operate in an environment analogous to CRM [customer relationship management], where information typically comes from only one or a handful of data sources that are then integrated into a single system or record (vs. CDI, which serves up information as required in true real time). Imagine the power of a CDI approach to look at supplier records from both internal systems and external content providers (even your supplier's systems) in real time vs. waiting for the next batch upload or data dump. This would provide an entirely new approach to looking at supplier information, one that paints a complete and accurate view of supplier data without creating a new system of record, providing potentially unprecedented real-time access to information that exists both within and without a company's four walls. It will also allow users to integrate new information sources in an often simple and rapid manner (vs. requiring underlying surgery, as it would in a database or data warehousing-centric approach).

---

[*] Handfield, *Supply Market Intelligence.*
[†] Busch, "Beyond the Basics."

Unfortunately, healthcare providers we interviewed are nowhere near having even basic spend analysis capabilities established. At its most basic level, a spend analysis solution should enable the capabilities shown in the matrix in Table 4.3 and answer the following questions:

1. Does the solution provide price benchmarking that is comparable not only to national pricing, but regional data, hospital size, and line item variance? Some of the solutions we examined provided benchmarking information, which was not linked with a spend management solution.

TABLE 4.3

Spend Analytics Capability Assessment

	Basic	**Typical**	**Advanced**
Price Benchmarking	National price benchmarking database. Printed, hard copy report	National price benchmarking database linked to hospital purchase data. Printed, hard copy report	National price benchmarking by hospital size and region linked to hospital purchase data for line-by-line variance. Online report with available export to Excel, PDF, or Word
Reports (based on part number)	Letter of Commitment Opportunity	Letter of Commitment Opportunity; Off-contract vendor purchases	Letter of Commitment Opportunity; Off-contract vendor purchases; PO discrepancy
Reports (based on commodity)	Data is aggregated by commodity	Data is aggregated by commodity, linked to purchase volumes	Data is aggregated by commodity, linked to purchase volumes and contracts, and used to examine on- and off-contract spend
Reports (based on charging)	Charge variance report that shows hospital where charge master is set inaccurately compared to varying purchase price	Charge variance report that shows hospital where charge master is set inaccurately compared to varying purchase price tied to purchase volume	Charge variance report that shows hospital where charge master is set inaccurately compared to varying purchase price tied to purchase volume and contracts

2. Does the solution provide spending analytics in a reporting format that can identify off-contract (e.g., maverick) spending, as well as discrepancies in purchase order contract pricing?

3. Does the solution provide reporting capabilities not only by commodity group, but linked to purchase volumes and spend leakage (e.g., maverick spending).

4. Does the solution provide reporting capabilities for charge variances linked to inaccurate master data (vs. variances in purchase volume and contract pricing)?

These capabilities are important to be able to not only identify the sources of spend leakage, but also to capture opportunities for improved leveraging and demand management. Demand management is the process of using unit and rate consumption levels to forecast and estimate the future consumption of an internal functional customer, provide guidance and input on how to optimize usage, and educate the user on the trade-offs. Demand management activities may involve (but are not limited to):*

- Optimization of sourcing strategies based on how much the team projects they will be buying
- Proactively setting policies, procedures, and measurement systems that throttle the consumption and total expenditures of a unit of category of spend
- Ensuring appropriate levels of capacity in the supply base required to minimize risk
- Establishing a fixed set of standards to limit options, and restricting the supply base to include only preferred suppliers who comply with risk and compliance requirements

The authority to review material specifications (and for services, a statement of work) is also within supply management's span of control in managing demand, although internal stakeholders sometimes dispute this right. Supply management personnel work hard to develop knowledge and expertise about a wide variety of materials and services, but must also make this knowledge work to an organization's benefit. The right to question allows supply management to review

---

* Handfield, *Supply Market Intelligence*.

specifications where required. In the case of services, it also allows supply management to ensure that the work being performed is correctly documented and performed. For example, sourcing managers may question whether a lower-cost item can still meet a physician's clinical requirement through proactive engagement of the physician team at a category team meeting. In documented cases identified by the author, proactive engagement of physicians in critical diagnosis-related group (DRG) areas such as hip and joint replacement can provide incredible cost and performance improvements.[*] They may also question the rate a consultant or maintenance provider is charging for a specific project or activity, and revise the work statement accordingly. A review of different requisitions may also reveal that different users actually require the same material or services. By combining purchase requirements, purchasing can often achieve a lower total cost. The reports generated from spend analysis and demand management provide a foundation for category management.

As shown in Figure 4.5, there are relatively few providers capable of providing a robust spend analysis reporting capability that meets all of these

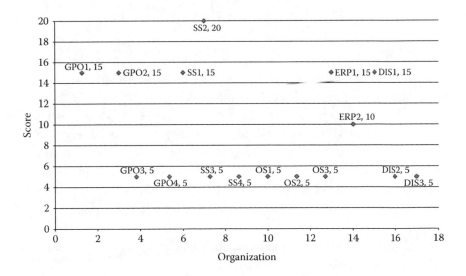

FIGURE 4.5
Spend analytics (max score = 20).

[*] Robert Handfield, PhD (Bank of America Professor of SCM), Tom Faciszewski MD and Thomas Nash, "Assessing Health Care Supply Chain Maturity: Creating a Baseline for Cost Savings, Value Creation and a Defined Structure for Growth," Keynote presentation, World Healthcare Congress, January 25, 2010.

requirements. The majority of providers are conducting data preparation activities, which does not enable clients to see the true output of the data cleansing exercise in a format that provides the reporting capabilities noted previously. If these providers are indeed capable of providing this capability, it remains a mystery as to why they are not selling the information back to the clients. In other words, the data preparation is focused exclusively on enabling their proprietary technology, which also ensures that the client will buy exclusively through their system to generate the revenue they require for their buying model. One of the distributors is selling an analytic tool that is focused on ensuring that the client will buy through them and save money.

Some of the other software providers (OS1, OS2, OS3) provided external price benchmarking data, but did not provide true analytics capabilities to clients, just a database of information. These trends were discovered through different interviews with industry subject matter experts. Unfortunately, we were not able to validate this view as our requests for demos and interviews were turned down. Only SS1 and SS2 were truly providing data cleansing and spend analytics solutions that met most of the basic criteria shown in the assessment.

Technology

The technology category consists of the different features and modes of presenting, reporting, and viewing spending metrics that are offered by any given solution provider. Personalized views for users, with multiple levels of analytic reports and the ability to export these reports to other tools for further analysis are important factors considered in evaluating provider technology. With technology comes the support function, the ability of vendors to provide dedicated support that looks to solve information technology, integration, and implementation issues.

A number of other factors can impact the relevant assessment of a provider's technology solution (see Table 4.4).

1. How easy is file maintenance? The core capability of the tool is the file maintenance dimension, the method of data extraction, and whether it is manual or automatic. The technology should enable data upload to both the customer's MMIS as well as the online portal on a regular basis, depending upon customer needs.

TABLE 4.4

Technology Capability Assessment

	Basic	Typical	Advanced
File maintenance	Data is manually sent in batches on an as-needed basis. Prepared reports are sent back to hospital.	Data extracts occur manually and are sent to vendor on a scheduled basis. Vendor uploads into the application and reports are available monthly or quarterly.	Automatic data extract, transfer, and loading to vendor with data returned to both the hospital for MMIS upload and uploaded into online reporting engine for productive use. Provides continuous contract and IM maintenance.
Ease of use	Application is installed at the hospital. Software requires a high degree of training. Hospital IT must be highly involved.	Application is either web based or hospital installed. Medium degree of training required to learn navigation. Hospital IT must be somewhat involved.	Application is web based with easy-to-use, intuitive functionality that multiple users with varying skill levels can understand. Administered by hospital power user. Hospital IT minimally involved.
Support	Application support is limited to e-mail with one- to three-day turnaround.	Help available via e-mail with one- to three-day turn-around or help desk during normal work hours.	Dedicated, ongoing relationship with implementation specialist during normal working hours. E-mail support with 24-hour turnaround.
Reporting data export function	Export capability limited to printing unformatted screens.	Reports are available in Excel with limited access to data within the application.	Report on all user-defined data can be exported in Excel, PDF, or Word format with icon-driven button click.

2. What is the technology's ease of use? How easy is it to use and interpret data? Is the technology web-enabled, with simple direct application methods? How involved does the client's internal IT function need to be?

3. What is the level of support provided by the provider? Ideally, e-mail support should have 24-hour turnaround, with dedicated individual support during implementation of the system.

4. What is the relative level of reporting capability? Does the system allow users to easily export data that can be manipulated in Excel, in PDF, and in Word formats at the click of a button?

Moreover, technology support is now a given for most systems, with clinicians and staff who now have little tolerance for screens and tools that are not readily user-friendly. Ideally, a standardized or virtual platform with tight processes, category, and functional integration can provide the level of technology and functionality that users have come to expect with most modern software systems.

This technology capability will become more important as users begin to apply data to other types of data capture, which can enable risk and supply market intelligence applications. Busch[*] notes how in the future users will be want to be able to combine different data elements and sources together via a supply risk mashup. (As background on this term, Wikipedia defines a mashup as "a web page or application that uses or combines data or functionality from two or many more external sources to create a new service.") Mashups can provide even more accurate insight into both overall (e.g., supplier viability) and narrowly tailored (e.g., potential for near-term disruption or material price increase) risk elements. Further, he notes how data download functionality will become more important, as increasingly savvy users will wish to rapidly drill down into an analysis to understand potential root causes of risk elements (e.g., a single-site supplier issue, logistical problems, underlying financial/working capital issues). This level of functionality will further enable users to bridge currently existing information silos/gaps among a variety of internal, supplier, and third-party information sources that are often defined by functional bounds; for example, the ability to integrate warranty claims data into a spend cube that also considers supplier financial viability or other elements.

Busch goes on to note:

Visualization and analytics technologies are also rapidly changing how we look at information. From emerging high-level dashboards that provide executive context and the ability to truly drill-into data that spans multiple source systems (e.g., A/P data, supplier provided data, P-Card data, VAT information, etc.) to analytical tools that allow sub-second response times when cross tabulating multiple variables (even dozens, in more extreme

---

[*] Jason Busch, "The Intersection of Analytics and Supply Chain Risk Management," *Spend Matters* Compass Series, Volume 1, 2010.

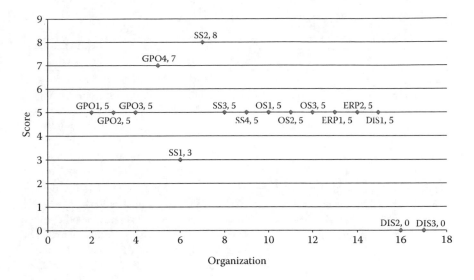

FIGURE 4.6
Technology (max score = 10).

cases), the entire foundation with which we have looked at original spend analysis approaches will eventually give way to a new generation of system. Today's handheld computing devices including iPhones and Blackberries often have 5,000 or more times the amount of main memory than personal computers. We will see an equal if not greater shift in the impact of how new technologies and query speeds will change spend analysis as we have in the power of PCs and portable devices.

As shown in Figure 4.6, the majority of providers have some level of capability relative to technology, but many lack the level of data export functionality. For the same reasons that the data cleansing exercise is limited, the willingness of firms to enable users to directly view and analyze the data for their own purposes is limited by design. One of the GPOs allows data export functionality to occur, but the majority of the firms consider the data to be proprietary and unavailable for querying, benchmarking, and analysis.

Service/Customer Responsiveness

Each company provides a customized application package with varying features that we have noted in prior sections. A fundamental requirement for all of the providers is the level of support and customer responsiveness that is experienced during not only implementation of the system,

TABLE 4.5

Service Capability Assessment

	Basic	Typical	Advanced
Materials consulting	Off-site nondedicated resource to support hospital personnel who are working reports	On-site dedicated resource to work reports	On-site dedicated resource to work reports, realign policies and procedures, and reengineer any processes resulting from the use of the technology
Technical consulting	Expertise to implement the vendor's application	Expertise to implement the application and to review its impact on other supply chain technology used by the hospital	Expertise to implement the application and to review its impact on other supply chain technology used by the hospital and support the data upload back into the MMIS
Validation and cultural change	Validation of application results performed by single employee within hospital materials department	Validation of application results and impact are performed by and overseen by a hospital multifunctional group	Validation of application results and impact are performed by and overseen by a hospital multifunctional group that examines associated cultural effects, processes, policies, and procedures

but ongoing technical support. The level of training and face time provided to employees who are new to the system can make the difference between a successful implementation and a failure. Ongoing support through e-mail or call center support is also critical to ongoing problem solving and user satisfaction with the system. In assessing this category, we considered the following questions, shown in Table 4.5.

1. Are on-site dedicated resources provided to assist users in learning how to use the reporting capability, as well as process redesign for any new spend management applications that are required in conjunction with system implementation?
2. Does the provider have on-site dedicated resources for technical consulting? Specifically, is a full systems assessment conducted to identify the impact of the technology on other supply chain technology within the impacted operating units, and is there support for ongoing data uploads on a regular basis to update the MMIS?

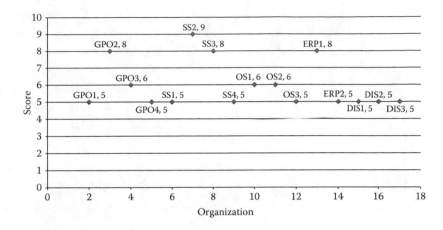

FIGURE 4.7
Service/responsiveness (max score = 10).

3. Does the provider support change management and buy-in for the system? This includes establishing a multifunctional governance team, validation of results achieved, and ongoing support for changes to policies and procedures?

The results in Figure 4.7 show that selected groups of GPOs, specialized software providers, and ERP providers do provide significant support. Many, however, fall short, especially with the level of on-site consulting and change management that is required to support change. The level of support needs to be identified and spelled out in detail prior to signing a contract with a provider, and specific elements of the validation deliverables need to be spelled out in detail.

Aggregate Score across Categories

Figure 4.8 provides a summary of the aggregated total score assigned to each of the providers reviewed in this assessment. Overall, only a single provider of integrated data cleansing, contract management, spend analytics, technology, and service stood out above the rest (SS2). While this provider did not receive a perfect score in each category, they exceeded the scores of other providers using the measurement rubric defined in this study.

The distribution of scores shows that only SS2 is capable of providing greater than 80% of the capabilities required for a thorough and complete spend management program. None of the other providers met the 60% threshold score, suggesting that healthcare providers using these

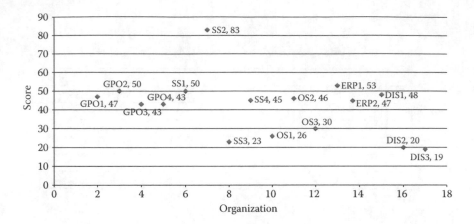

FIGURE 4.8
Total score (max score = 100).

solutions are not benefiting from the power of a thorough and complete spend management program. The fundamental issues that most healthcare providers ignore when selecting a provider are data quality and data ownership and analytics. Many providers claim to have a cleansing function that will ensure data quality. In effect, data cleansing is the primary step and the most important one if a healthcare provider is seeking to automate its data management process. This step will determine the accuracy of all ensuing analysis of information, which will impact category strategies, contracting, and supplier relationship management. Without a proper data cleansing effort, follow-on activities occur in a void.

This was emphasized in an interview with one of the subject matter experts identified in this study. He noted that different providers do indeed have different capabilities related to different components of spend management. Although many healthcare providers have similar issues pertaining to supply management, they need to be able to link their strategies to other areas such as clinical professionals, finance, human resources, IT, and other functional areas. Often supply chain functionality is assumed to exist under the large system requirements provided by ERP systems, GPO solutions, or distributor systems, and there is a belief that these packages can provide a single solution to the problem. Our results suggest that this perception is without merit, and that further engagement of alternative providers that specialize in data cleansing, coding, and capture may provide greater benefits than GPOs and ERP vendors who do not have strong capabilities in this arena.

CONCLUSION

The concept of strategic sourcing has been well touted in the industry as a core tool for hospital IDNs to achieve their clinical mission while managing risk and reducing cost. One of the most fundamental components of a strategic sourcing program is the ability to carry out a category analysis for consolidated spend data at the hospital, as well as at the buyer level.* This requires aggregating 100% of the data into a single consolidated view of the spend data to enable a precise analysis of spending with each supplier for each category of spend in the system.

In this study, we surveyed the landscape of different providers of spend management in the healthcare landscape. This included GPOs, ERP system providers, specialized software providers, and distributors. The five major categories of spend management assessed at each of these organizations includes data cleansing, spend analytics, contract management, technology enablement, and customer service/responsiveness. Of these, data cleansing was identified as the most challenging component that is fundamental to creating true visibility of spend. Unfortunately, data cleansing is also the component that was typically overlooked by the majority of the organizations reviewed in this analysis. While each of these information system providers facilitates a different and unique set of capabilities in the area of contract management, technology, analytics, and support, only two of the providers truly have a demonstrated capability in capturing, cleansing, coding, and uploading 100% of the spend data for hospitals and IDNs. Further, many of the organizations perform data cleansing only as a requirement for entering the data into their proprietary databases, without providing the cleansed dataset to the client. Without capturing and providing visibility to 100% of the spend (including not just EDI data, but non-EDI spending, paper contracts, off-system spending, etc.), the true benefits of a strategic sourcing exercise cannot be achieved, and the result is a self-defeating exercise in futility. Only two providers of specific software targeted at data cleansing were identified in the study. This was made more complicated by the fact that up to 20% of manufacturer data that are used as input into healthcare data analysis are "dirty" or incorrect.

In today's environment, hospitals continue to outsource their sourcing capabilities to a national or regional group of GPOs that are able to obtain

---

* Schneller, "A Guide to Successful Strategic Sourcing."

leveraged savings for groups of large commodities. In this environment, many providers are not highly motivated to look for other avenues of savings beyond price, and are ignoring the power of strategies such as demand management, clinical effectiveness, and engagement of stakeholders in the sourcing process. Further, healthcare providers remain largely unaware of their needs and requirements, and rely on these third parties to perform data cleansing and analysis, trusting them to act in their best interests (which in some cases are not aligned with the third party's internal strategic revenue objectives). The general experience has been that hospitals and IDNs want one package tool that takes care of all the issues. To truly assume a strategic leadership role, however, healthcare supply chain executives need to adopt a strategic intent to insist on visibility and cleanliness of all data, not just what is easily accessible. Further, the data need to be captured in an analytical environment that allows the flexibility to drill deeply into different types of datasets to unearth opportunities through benchmarking, comparative cost effectiveness studies analysis of nontraditional spending areas, and engagement of key stakeholders to review the results of these analyses. Data are the only true enablers for change in the healthcare supply chain. Our research points to the need for strategic sourcing groups across the country to begin to take the issue of spend management into their own hands, control the data, and use them as leveraged tools for driving change and improving performance.

Gene Schneller, in a recent article, emphasizes that perhaps it is naïve to believe that supply chain managers in U.S. hospitals will become strategic sourcing experts.* Although GPOs are taking the lead in supply management to begin providing contracting solutions to the spend management challenges that exist in many healthcare environments, and GPO solutions are certainly a good start, the solutions offered by GPOs may not provide the full extent of leverage and performance improvements that healthcare providers could achieve through alternative solutions. Specifically, these opportunities can be enabled through improved visibility of spend data. This development will be further enabled through the development of standards such as GS1, which provides a more robust platform for standardization.

In the short term, however, our analysis suggests that specialized providers can work closely with healthcare providers to gain more control over their spending. Data cleansing solutions that provide visibility to current spending, including paper contracts and non-EDI data can

---

* Schneller, "A Guide to Successful Strategic Sourcing."

provide a holistic view of current spend, and provide a solid platform for analytics, contract management, technology enablement, and most importantly, supply and market intelligence. In viewing the full extent and nature of spending patterns, supply chain managers can begin to analyze and explore these datasets, linking them with other data in the organization, to create a powerful mechanism for opportunity identification. Busch[*] notes that when conducted thoroughly, spend management enables firms to:

- Gain directional indications of where the best opportunities may come from based on initial benchmarking exercises and potentially third-party category analysis
- Create a spend visibility toolset that enables viewing of both PO and non-PO information
- Develop strategies to integrate nontraditional datasets into a spend analysis environment (e.g., legal, marketing, clinical, and related systems data)
- Perform more sophisticated analyses using local tools and methods, including what-if scenarios, risk analyses, and budget forecasts based on market intelligence studies
- Engage executive champions in the system (e.g., CFO, COO, clinician counsels) that will submit their own information for analysis and review, including tax, audit, financial and clinical performance, and DRG cost analysis (more than fifty DRG groups have costs of supplies plus operating room time exceeding half the total cost of admission)

When sourcing begins to drive strategies based on data, not just opinion, they will be surprised at the power of this data as strong components for change. Clinicians and CFOs are by their very nature convinced to change when confronted with validated data that cannot be refuted. A strong spend management program will not only elevate the strategic position of sourcing executives in healthcare, but create opportunities for sourcing executives to accomplish these goals:

- Contribute to budgets and business plans based on overall business impact, not just category cost savings or labor efficiency gains.

---

[*] Busch, "Beyond the Basics."

- Leverage the data to radically alter clinical processes, DRG procedures, and other processes that may be broken or inconsistently performed, thereby increasing clinical effectiveness.
- Provide technologies and solutions to users throughout the system that will increase efficiencies, reduce internal cosourcing efforts, and reduce not just labor costs but working capital.
- Leverage third-party service firms not just for systems selection and implementation, but for process knowledge transfer. Third-party suppliers can be engaged to identify opportunities for further improvement and cost savings through improved supplier relationships.

All of this requires healthcare organizations to select providers who are aligned with a spend management strategy that relies on centralization of spending and engagement of stakeholders for decision making. Procurement business process outsourcing has become the norm in healthcare. It's time to regain internal control of spend data and begin to truly manage third-party spending as a strategic capability. While strategic sourcing has grown by leaps and bounds in most industries, healthcare has a long way to go. The time for change has never been better.

APPENDIX: SUPPLIER SCORE CARD KEY

	Basic	Typical	Advanced
Item master build	Accepts current item master file as is.	Collects MMIS purchase order, and item master file analyzes by spend, and delivers result to hospital.	Collects core files from all supply chain departments, analyzes by spend, and consults with hospital on final item master file.
Verification of distributor catalog number, manufacturer, manufacturer catalog number, catalog description, and packaging data	Data is normalized in its current state without reference to an existing database.	Matches precleansed data to an existing database. Unmatched has no action taken. Packaging accepted at purchase UOM.	Matches precleansed data to an existing database. Unmatched manually verified at product source. Packaging researched to low UOM.

	Basic	Typical	Advanced
Description standardization	Reorganization of current client description to follow vendor-decided naming convention.	Rules and abbreviations are provided by vendor with standard schema for use with every client.	Rules and abbreviations are customizable per client needs. Vendor has clinicians write descriptions.
Item classification	Applies a proprietary classification schema not based on an external standard.	Applies UNSPSC codes to items.	Applies UNSPSC codes to items and provides clinical equivalency.
Physical copies of contracts are available in application	Contracts are in a searchable archive with limited vendor predefined search criteria.	Contracts are in a searchable archive with multiple vendor predefined search criteria.	Contracts are in a searchable archive with multiple vendor predefined search criteria as well as custom hospital specific criteria (e.g., department and buyer codes).
Contract types handled	GPO only.	GPO contracts but locals manually uploaded by hospital with limited access.	Contract warehouse holds any type of contract (e.g., GPO, local, and nonsupply).
Reporting capability	User can obtain reports on a single group of GPO contracts.	Reporting available by contract class, type, and OEM on GPO contracts only.	Robust reporting of all supply contracts by type, buyer, date, OEM, class, tiers, rebates, renewal, etc.
Item-level detail	Items are tied to contracts. Search is limited to contract header or contract name for GPO contracts only.	Items are tied to contracts. Search is limited to contract header or contract name for GPO and local contracts.	Contract warehouse is searchable by item-level detail using OEM or distributor information and reports across all contracts local and GPO.

(Continued)

	Basic	Typical	Advanced
Ease of use	Application is installed at the hospital. Software requires a high degree of training. Hospital IT must be highly involved.	Application is either web based or hospital installed. Medium degree of training required to learn navigation. Hospital IT must be somewhat involved.	Application is web based with easy-to-use, intuitive functionality that multiple users with varying skill levels can understand. Administered by hospital power user. Hospital IT minimally involved.
Support	Application support is limited to e-mail with one- to three-day turnaround.	Help available via e-mail with one- to three-day turnaround or help desk during normal work hours.	Dedicated, ongoing relationship with implementation specialist during normal working hours. E-mail support with 24-hour turnaround.
Reporting data export function	Export capability limited to printing unformatted screens.	Reports are available in Excel with limited access to data within the application.	Report on all user-defined data can be exported in Excel, PDF, or Word format with icon-driven button click.
Price benchmarking	National price benchmarking database. Printed, hard copy report.	National price benchmarking database linked to hospital purchase data. Printed, hard copy report.	National price benchmarking by hospital size and region linked to hospital purchase data for line-by-line variance. Online report with available export to Excel, PDF, or Word.
Reports (based on part number)	Letter of Commitment Opportunity.	Letter of Commitment Opportunity; off-contract vendor purchases.	Letter of Commitment Opportunity; off-contract vendor purchases; PO discrepancy.

(*Continued*)

	Basic	Typical	Advanced
Reports (based on commodity)	Data is aggregated by commodity.	Data is aggregated by commodity, linked to purchase volumes.	Data is aggregated by commodity, linked to purchase volumes and contracts, and used to examine on- and off-contract spend.
Reports (based on charging)	Charge variance report that shows hospital where charge master is set inaccurately compared to varying purchase price.	Charge variance report that shows hospital where charge master is set inaccurately compared to varying purchase price tied to purchase volume.	Charge variance report that shows hospital where charge master is set inaccurately compared to varying purchase price tied to purchase volume and contracts.
Materials consulting	Off-site nondedicated resource to support hospital personnel who are working reports.	On-site dedicated resource to work reports.	On-site dedicated resource to work reports, realign policies and procedures, and reengineer any processes resulting from the use of the technology.
Technical consulting	Expertise to implement the vendor's application	Expertise to implement the application and to review its impact on other supply chain technology used by the hospital.	Expertise to implement the application and to review its impact on other supply chain technology used by the hospital and support the data upload back into the MMIS.
Validation and cultural change	Validation of application results performed by single employee within hospital materials department.	Validation of application results and impact are performed by and overseen by a hospital multifunctional group.	Validation of application results and impact are performed by and overseen by a hospital multifunctional group that examines associated cultural effects, processes, policies, and procedures.

5

Electronic Collaboration in
Life Sciences Supply Networks

INTRODUCTION

The biopharmaceutical industry is faced with an increasing set of challenges. Worldwide, pharmaceutical and biotech companies are under increasing pressure to develop, produce, and deliver more products. As one executive noted:

> The challenge is straightforward: supply more quality drugs to more people in a shorter period of time—at a profit to one's company and at minimal risk to the end user. But with rising development costs, pressing regulatory compliance issues, fierce competition, price controls, advanced technological concerns, and the integration of compliance and validation systems into the infrastructure of worldwide manufacturing plants, this challenge calls for a complicated balancing act that requires a lot of players.[*]

Pharmaceutical companies have sought to acquire more companies in the biologics space, to drive increased pipeline selection, expanded product distribution systems, ability to create therapeutic franchises, greater market presence, and an accumulation of applied best-practice knowledge. The desired results can be extremely beneficial, specifically in these areas: accelerated development and approval of pipeline products, expanded multinational launches in-licensing, deeper market penetration, improved life-cycle management, intellectual property utilization, and improved inventory management.[†] Further, more and more companies are outsourcing to contract manufacturing and packaging organizations and expanding

---

[*] Trish Ellis, "Are You Ready for Global Manufacturing?" *Pharmaceutical Technology* 25, no. 9 (2001): 86–90.
[†] Gil Bashe, "Global Branding Challenge," *Pharmaceutical Executive* 20, no. 6 (2000): 72–79.

their reach to global sales channels. The trend toward outsourcing on the demand side is occurring because of the following major challenges:

1. The U.S. domestic market is becoming increasingly saturated, so that going global is one of the few remaining ways to grow;
2. The pressures of managed care in the United States are making it more difficult to increase sales of products that do not have demonstrated outcomes advantages when compared with available lower-priced alternatives; and
3. New drugs and medical devices can be marketed and accepted outside of the United States much more quickly than within the United States, so that new product launches and sales can take place months or years earlier if a company plans globally.[*]

To summarize, some of the key constraints faced by pharmaceutical manufacturers include:

- **Slowing growth:** Overall industry growth is slowing, both globally and in the developed U.S. and European Union (EU) markets.
- **Shifting geographical markets:** Growth is shifting from mature markets to emerging markets.
- **Shifting care markets:** The traditional focus on broad scope primary care blockbusters is shifting to specialist-driven, therapeutically targeted products.
- **Shifting product line mix:** Biotech and generics product line growth is outstripping branded small-molecule big pharma growth.
- **Existing financial model threatened:** Significant revenue and shareholder value is being threatened by large-scale patent losses and pricing pressures due to a focus on lowering health care costs.

On the supply side, the drive to efficiently access global materials markets, simplify and shorten supply chains to local and regional markets, as well as a desire to cut operational costs, have also incented biopharma firms to outsource more and more of their supply chain processes to third-party contract manufacturing organizations, bulk manufacturers, clinical trials organizations, and third-party logistics providers.[†] The total level of production

---

[*] Elaine Whitmore, *Product Development Planning for Health Care Products Regulated by the FDA* (Milwaukee, WI: ASQC Quality Press, 1997).
[†] Ibid.

being outsourced has risen from approximately 20% (by volume) in 2005 to over 35% in 2011 and the trend line continues to rise.

Unfortunately, outsourcing brings with it numerous other challenges that are often unforeseen. For example, prior research identifies multiple challenges associated with clinical trials of new products globally: recruiting patients is becoming increasingly difficult, and companies are recruiting in clinics all over the world in an attempt to speed up the velocity of these trials in a race to the market. In the process, the challenges associated with developing appropriate comparators, Interactive Voice Response (IVRS) systems development, recruiting patients, planning lead times, and getting the product to the right location, with the right regulatory requirements, right label, right instructions, and right doses is an incredible challenge.

Our current research further documents the challenges of managing end-to-end supply chains, with an emphasis on the material supply, manufacturing, and packaging ecosystem. The study also discusses data that suggests the need for integrating data systems, standardizing processes, and creating strategic and collaborative customer–supplier relationships to achieve success. There is a strong need for executives in buying and selling organizations to work together more closely to ensure quality and regulatory compliance, on-time delivery, and patient care in the supply chain environment.

In this study, we review the following components of our research:

- Methodology
- The state of the biopharmaceutical supply chain ecosystem
- The current state of electronic collaboration
- Gaps in forecasting and planning capabilities
- Major gaps in electronic collaboration today
- Key priorities for improvement
- Solution characteristics
- Potential benefits of investment in collaborative technologies
- Insights and recommendations for the future

METHODOLOGY FOR THE STUDY

This study was conducted in order to further explore the following areas of inquiry identified by biopharma firms and care management organization/care plan oversight Contract Manufacturing/Contract Research Outsource

(CMO/CRO) partners who, faced with an increasingly complex set of outsourcing and product relationships, wished to identify approaches to integrate this network.

- What are the attributes of an optimized supply network in this industry?
- In which business areas could companies collaborate?
- Where do they actually collaborate today and at what level?
- On which operational processes within these areas should they collaborate?
- On which processes do they collaborate today and at what level?
- What measurable benefit would this provide?
- What data are required to support the optimum collaborative network?
- What level of data access is currently available?

The study began with a series of detailed interviews with subject matter experts at seven biopharma companies and three contract manufacturers.

Following these interviews, a survey was designed and sent to 950 executives at biopharma companies. A total of 126 executives responded to the survey. These responses were a reasonable sample, providing views from a variety of industry participants, including both large pharmaceutical companies with annual revenue of over $5 billion, to medium- and small-sized pharmaceutical and biopharmaceutical companies with annual revenue of less than $1 billion. Contract manufacturers and packagers surveyed also spanned the range from over $1 billion in annual revenue to less than $100 million in annual revenue. Respondents were primarily from supply chain and IT roles, although a number of other business functions (quality, business development, procurement, etc.) were also represented.

In the remainder of the chapter, we capture the key trends extracted from these interviews and survey respondents.

Biopharmaceutical Ecosystem

Observation: Customer products and markets are ramping up in complexity, but current forms of collaboration are unable to cope with the need to manage this complexity.

In all of the interviews and survey results, we identified increasing complexity as a fact of life. Customers are experiencing more globalization of their supply base as they are being pushed into supplying products to emerging markets with immature supply chain infrastructures. Because there are not as many blockbusters due to the efficiency of generics, the dynamics of product supply needs are changing. An escalation in mergers and acquisitions is further muddying the planning capabilities, due to greater numbers of legacy systems, misaligned planning capabilities, and new inherited products. Regulatory requirements are coming down the pipeline with track and trace, and serialization. On top of this, the threats of counterfeiting, reimbursement fraud, patient safety concerns in multiple government milieus, and raw material origin concerns, have created an unprecedented situation. People in the biopharma supply chain are being challenged at a level that hasn't been seen before. This has made the old systems of communication (e-mail, fax, and phone) not only inefficient, but a major threat to business continuity in the face of this complexity.

The survey results that examine this environmental complexity are shown in Figure 5.1. In general, almost 80% of companies agree that complexity is occurring on many fronts, including increasing globalization of supply, increased packaging complexity and regulatory controls, and operational complexity due to mergers. About two-thirds of companies face increased complexity due to targeted therapies and markets, as well as products with shorter production runs and smaller lot sizes.

As shown in Figure 5.2, this complexity is getting worse as the number of external relationships (customers, CMOs/CPOs, and material suppliers) in the supply chain explodes. Managing relationships in a "one-off" fashion

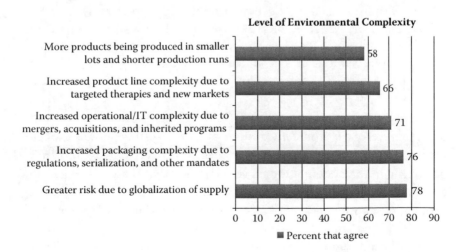

Level of Environmental Complexity

FIGURE 5.1
The global biopharmaceutical ecosystem is becoming more complex and riskier.

Average Number of CMOs/CPOs	37
Number of material suppliers for buying companies	10s to 100s
Number of customers for CMO/CPO	10s to 1000s
Share of production outsourced by buying companies	39%
Share of production PLANNED for outsourcing	39%

FIGURE 5.2
A growing amount of production is occurring in an outsourced or virtual environment.

is impossible, and gaining efficiency via "private" networks fails when a company ends up participating in dozens of private networks.

Despite this increasingly difficult ecosystem, biopharmaceutical companies have fallen behind in their ability to listen and respond to the fluctuations and global requirements of the rapidly changing supply chain. Specifically, more than 80% of executives agree that almost no transparency exists across the production life cycle, and that little to no collaboration occurs during execution of production processes. This comment comes from a leading CMO:

> Our customers are experiencing complexity that has never been seen in the history of the industry. The way we work with our customers today is a labor-intensive, ad hoc method of phone, fax, e-mail, and face to face, with large amounts of data transfer through spreadsheets and CSV [comma-separated values] files. Because this is the way we've always done it, everyone thinks it is acceptable. Quite honestly, it is not. We have to find ways to communicate data in a more efficient and timely manner, and for the data to be shared and communized to both entities at the same time.

Further, the level of shared access to real-time production and supply data, the level of electronic integration, and the resulting poor level of planning on shared production processes means there are massive *disconnects* occurring in the system. Our surveys confirm that there is a huge gap in capability that exists today, and this was made even more tangible through some of the comments shared by executives with whom we spoke:

> Our planning process desperately needs more discipline. It was being managed on a tight cash flow basis. That is well and good when you have high forecast accuracy and consistent demand, which we did with two

mature products in three countries. But in the last five years, our product portfolio has increased and we have nine or ten different SKUs [stock keeping units] per presentation, and massive expansion into new markets with poor forecast accuracy, with considerably smaller sales volumes. And then you overlay parallel trade in our European markets, and it becomes even more difficult. (Mid-sized Biopharma)

We have so many things coming together, not just drug product. Whether it is in fill-finish or packaging, we have to coordinate empty syringes, cartons, and other ancillary items. So if there is a stock situation with one element of supply (quality rejections, or late deliveries, or mismanagement by a CMO), the entire order is delayed. (Mid-sized Biopharma)

I have eleven commercialized drugs and relationships with eighteen different contract manufacturers due to inherited or acquired programs. We need to have some strategic thinking about what our strategy should be, but in the meantime this is what we have to deal with. Many of these relationships are with companies who have very immature planning processes. (Leading Biopharma)

With the merger mania that has been occurring with many big customers, customers are encountering major issues as they try to get their cultural blending in line, and figure out how to run their supply chains. This has caused a greater degree of unpredictability in the channel. As soon as we discover a problem or a major deviation, we contact them and ensure that we are transparent about how we can manage the issue, or at least notify the customer early on and have a lively exchange on the subject. But this occurs through phone or e-mail, not in real time. (Top-5 CMO)

Observation: Product serialization will further complicate the situation. Another important trend that is driving problems is track and trace/serialization regulations. This is a serious issue. Over twenty states in the United States alone have some measure of track and trace regulation, along with multiple other countries around the globe. This adds a new set of CMO–Pharma–Distribution relationships that need to be managed.

We believe there is a need for a process link which is around the receipt of serialization numbers from our customers into SAP, deployment to shop floor, application to packs, reconciliation and tracking of numbers used versus destroyed. The only way this will work is some form of electronic link in the cloud. (Top-5 CMO)

We are looking for a different system is because of serialization requirements. This is a hard stopping point that can't be done manually, which requires a level of information and detail and accuracy which is critical. If we are working with multiple CMOs and have to put a unique ID on every bottle of drug, then we have to be able to generate blocks of numbers to these CMOs. We can't let them generate random numbers on their own. So we need a centralized approach of getting serial numbers to people and companies, but it is only during manufacturing and packaging that you have visibility to these numbers and how they are used and applied. We are talking about cases and cases of pallets—and that is the kind of data we have to get into our system! (Leading Pharma)

We believe the biotech field may be more interested in the quality link than the serialization link. The number of transactions with biotech is smaller, and the transaction piece is less important to them than the quality piece. On the other hand, generics are very hot on serialization, while pharma is interested in order transaction visibility. So we need to start segmenting these markets. (Leading Biopharma)

Part number differences are a big problem. We have our own internal item classification for every item we produce but it doesn't necessarily carry over to our third-party providers. So there needs to be some sort of conversion process. (Leading Biopharma)

One of the biggest drivers of problems is complexity. One company has a standard fermentation batch, but what changes consistently are the twenty-six country configurations. We find that pharma companies often have good primary costs, but secondary costs are spiraling due to country complexity. If things are not working well, then why not?

What Is the State of Electronic Collaboration in Biopharma?

In many industries, *collaboration* is a term that is generally overused. Two useful definitions of collaboration include the following:

- working together to achieve a goal, and
- a recursive process where two or more people or organizations work together to realize shared goals.

In the sense of electronic collaboration, biopharma companies seek to work with their CMOs or other suppliers to achieve specific objectives or goals. In most cases, this is toward timely, accurate, and responsive delivery of products and services. Although this is certainly being achieved to some extent today, the means to do so is highly inefficient.

In virtually every one of the companies we spoke with, planning was supported by an array of individuals armed with Excel spreadsheets, telephones, faxes, and travel schedules (Figure 5.3). Almost all data

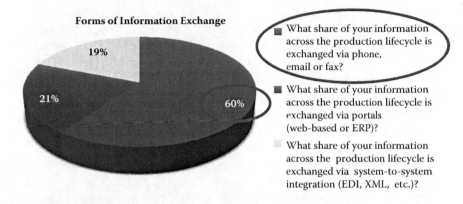

Forms of Information Exchange

19%

21%

60%

- What share of your information across the production lifecycle is exchanged via phone, email or fax?

- What share of your information across the production lifecycle is exchanged via portals (web-based or ERP)?

- What share of your information across the production lifecycle is exchanged via system-to-system integration (EDI, XML, etc.)?

FIGURE 5.3
One key reason is that the supply network information foundation doesn't support growing industry requirements.

exchange and planning was being done on Excel spreadsheets, with a few exceptions of companies who had achieved Class A Manufacturing Resource Planning (MRP) II status. This was also validated by the results of our survey, which shows that two thirds of respondents still rely on phone, e-mail, or fax for communication about production execution. Another 21% utilize some form of web-based portal that is proprietary to the specific relationship, while 19% utilize some electronic format of electronic data interchange (EDI) or extensible markup language (XML).

There were two other major problems noted by managers who had already invested in some form of portal or EDI capability:

1. The average length of time for firms to map, build, and test an operational EDI link was about six months.
2. This link was exclusive to one specific supply relationship. A single supplier may have requests from many different customers to use their proprietary enterprise resource planning (ERP) system or exchange system, so this plurality of systems caused major headaches, limited reuse, and eliminated any scale efficiencies that might arise.

This was reflected by several of the comments made by executives we interviewed.

We actually do have a lot of visibility, but we have had to invest massive resources into making sure that we don't make mistakes. We have a whole department of twelve people whose sole responsibility is to manage CMOs, and obtain updates through e-mails, phone calls, and spreadsheets. If someone doesn't come to work, we're behind. And we do almost everything internally, including our own sampling, etc. We ignore any third parties that could do it for us. And we can't allocate until it goes through all of the Quality review. (Leading Pharma)

Because many of our customers require it, we know we have to have integrity in our supply chain. We will take them though an exercise of value stream mapping. This is common in many industries, but we cannot assume that customers are aware of it. This can raise certain issues, such as mapping cycle times and inventories, and there is an educational aspect to this. (Top-5 CMO)

The complexity can increase pretty quickly and escalates into a real mess. We have companies that give us between fifteen and thirty pages of spread-sheets with their latest forecasts—and then it gets interesting. (Top-5 CMO)

I found it interesting in talking to people that we were the same as everyone else! Before, I used to think we were the exception rather than the rule in terms of our ability to get data [in] real time. But since then I have learned that even the large pharma companies are challenged with this, even though they are more advanced than we are in supply chain best practices. I think it is a function of the internal CMO managers' capabili-ties, and that is more of a manual process regardless of who is doing it. (Leading Biopharma)

We created an internal system which extracted information out of SAP on a daily basis, loaded it into a flat file, and sent it to them. This local spoke solution worked quite well as a way to share information but has become cumbersome not only to set up. We know that suppliers are on the receiving end of twenty different ways to collaborate from other customers. We also use SharePoint and e-Rooms, but this is also very static information. (Leading Pharma)

We do have one site that has an electronic connection into our ERP system. That is it. Ninety percent of the rest of it is done manually. (Leading Pharma)

The survey results in the area of data sharing and collaborative process execution highlighted in Figure 5.4 demonstrate the low level of maturity and high level of fragmentation across the industry in this area. Less than 20% of companies say that they enjoy full electronic integration with exter-nal partners and customers, and less than 15% have the level of end-to-end transparency that they desire across the production lifecycle.

In addition, as demonstrated in Figure 5.5, more than half of supply chain partners use different data formats for production and supply information, more than half use different business-to-business (B2B) technology and

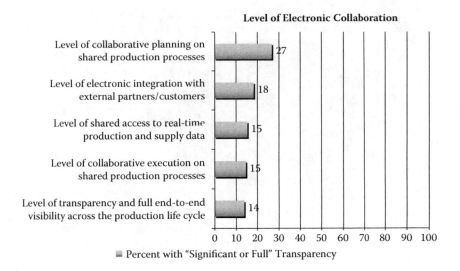

FIGURE 5.4
There is a significant barrier to supply network collaboration across the industry.

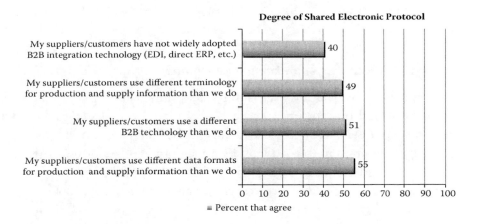

FIGURE 5.5
Improving this information exchange foundation is key, but is challenging given the diversity of the network.

more than half use different supply chain terminology. Although a lack of common nomenclature and systems standards is certainly a problem, it is amazing that 40% of companies note that their customers or suppliers have not widely adopted any form of electronic integration technology. Phone, e-mail, fax, and paper flow still predominate as the glue and baling wire that holds together most supply network relationships.

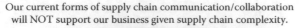

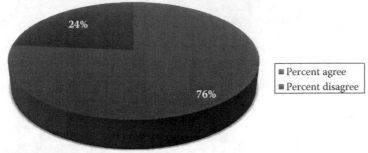

FIGURE 5.6
The result is a general agreement that the current way of sharing information and process collaboration will not serve the life science supply network going forward.

Thus, it is not surprising that the great majority of both biopharma and contract partner respondents stated that their current infrastructure for data sharing and process collaboration will not support their companies appropriately in the future global business environment (see Figure 5.6).

Dearth of Forecasting and Planning Capabilities

Unfortunately, the data suggest that forecasting and planning capabilities are not only lacking, but are largely absent in many current supply chain relationships today. Both customers and suppliers emphasized that forecasting capabilities are typically off by a magnitude of 20%–50%. There is also a trend that variation is greatest for product in the initial stages of the product launch. While customers are generally good at supporting the technology transfer and putting information into a common technical document (CTD), there is a massive variation in the ability of customers to forecast well.

Very few companies in this space have achieved Class A MRP certification, which provides the fundamental stepping stones for effective forecasting, sales and operations planning, inventory and safety stock calculations, and global production planning. Without this foundational base, communication of requirements between life sciences' companies and CMOs is increasingly erratic. In many cases, companies are taking information from their international markets and attempting to compound them into an Excel spreadsheet, and the ability to produce

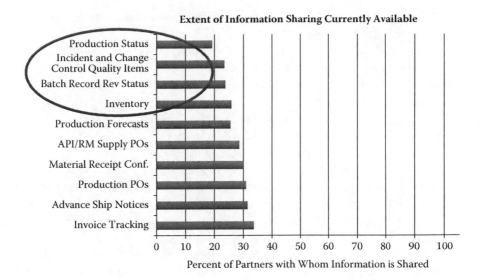

Extent of Information Sharing Currently Available

Percent of Partners with Whom Information is Shared

FIGURE 5.7
The reality today is that manufacturing and supply chain process data are infrequently shared.

any type of forecast, let alone an eighteen-month rolling SKU forecast, is impossible.

The survey results suggest that not only is the level of shared information low, but what little information is shared is restricted to primarily transactional data, not forecasting, inventory, or production status (see Figure 5.7). In fact, less than 25% of companies share any form of inventory, production forecast, or batch record review status with their partners. This lack of visibility creates havoc with supply planning and production schedules, as noted by several of the interviewed executives:

> I am happy to live with 90% forecast accuracy over a twelve-month window. But most customers barely hit 70%. And we always have to remind them to give the forecast to us as they forget! In many cases it is because they have different marketing people who give us forecasts based on their best guess, not based on any formal system. (Leading Pharma)
>
> We have approximately ninety–one hundred client relationships, and serve nineteen of the top twenty big pharma companies in the world. Few of these companies have basic planning capabilities, and in many cases, doesn't even exist. Out of this top twenty, only 50% have Class A certification. Three that I know of routinely provide us with forecasting information that will be completely inaccurate, and our team knows to automatically adjust these forecasts based on prior experience. Then you

throw in the possibility of a major disruption—and everything goes haywire. (Top-5 CMO)

We ask for a twenty four-month rolling forecast visibility in the hope we might get eighteen or twelve. If we ask for twelve, we will get nine or six, even though all of our forecasts require a twelve-month forecast. We do our scheduling and planning against the three-month firm period the customer's forecast is showing us, but there is always a question market on the customer's forecast accuracy and whether we will get the PO [purchase order] by the end of the given month. (Leading CMO)

I came from high tech, and what I encountered in biopharma is that there is a very limited use of MRP and little understanding of planning. This was characterized by little concern over the cost of inventory, and little focus on cost and rudimentary planning. In electronics contract manufacturing we utilized systems to drive visibility of inventory everywhere in the pipeline. But in life sciences, even though we own inventory, there is limited management of inventory. My objective is to create a planning culture with a sense of urgency and documented tight-knit processes. But I have learned it also takes time to get things done and responsiveness isn't cultural. (Leading Biopharma)

Information Gaps in Current Electronic Collaboration

Many of the companies we spoke with identified that data asymmetry and missing data was a common problem, followed by timeliness of data. Both suppliers and customers pointed to each other as the source of the problem. Executives were quick to react and point the finger at the other party, noting how they either were "not responsive," or alternatively, "didn't give us the right information." However, progressive companies recognize the importance of regular, shared reviews of performance rather than blaming first before understanding.

We believe a good place to start is to identify the *gaps* in information required to make better decisions. Then, prioritize these gaps and identify the type of information required, where it comes from, and then map out a process to collect and disseminate the information on a regularly planned schedule.

The survey results point to some obvious gaps to close. The biggest gap is around execution. Information on current production status, inventory status, quality status, batch record review status, and material receipt confirmation is at the top of the list in terms of gaps between current performance and importance to improve (Figure 5.8).

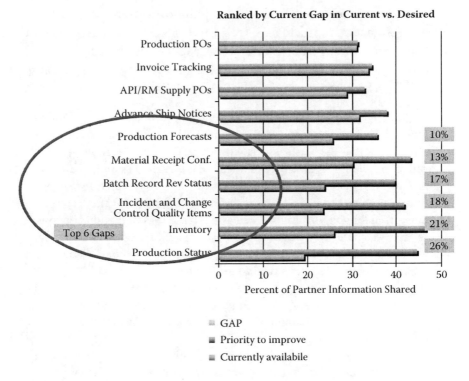

FIGURE 5.8
Leaders are generally dissatisfied with their visibility of and access to timely data as a basis for multi-enterprise collaboration.

> One of the things we face is that our customers send us orders—but not their active ingredients to make it. So when we are late, they conveniently forget that we didn't have the Active Pharmaceutical Ingredient (API) for them. (Leading CMO)
>
> The biggest problems are around planning information, including demand and forecast, as well as quality information. We need to share this information to enable people to make decisions on our behalf, rather than us having to do it for them. There is also a need to be able to track change, especially in a packaging environment where you have a large number of SKUs due to frequent market changes. We need to get visibility of that information to our suppliers. (Leading Pharma)

These gaps are also the same items that are on the "fast track" priority to improve. All parties expressed a need for a solution that could drive information visibility to all parties in a secure environment. Ideally, such a system would allow parties to connect in the cloud, map ERP data tables into the cloud, and allow customers to pull down from the cloud their specific transactional data to have real-time visibility and shared visibility of their transactional data. Conversely, CMOs would be able to receive POs from the customers' ERP system that flow into their system, along with order acknowledgment, sales orders, work orders, and so on.

> Wouldn't it be great if our customers could get production status visibility without having to call us or send an e-mail! They could see a traffic light with a status that the batch associated with a PO number is in dispensing, production quality, or quality review—or wherever in the supply chain! We are willing to open the kimono and let our customers have full transparency around anything having to do with their orders. For instance, they could see days outstanding on invoices, as well as the trend on whether it is improving, and we could have some really constructive discussions around that data and around performance. We want to increase collaboration because that is where you can differentiate yourself as a supplier. (Top-5 CMO)
>
> One of the key issues is that once a product gets into the clean room and is sitting there as inventory, it is supposed to be the end of the story. But one of the downsides is around deviations caused by things that are unexpected. (Top-5 CMO)
>
> It would be good if we could include FedEx or UPS tracking in addition to other information on the batch. This is especially the case when we drop into depots in exotic locations, where we need to understand the status of the delivery as well as the inventory position. (Leading Biopharma)
>
> You need to have personal information to get accurate information. Someone is always overshooting or being too conservative—and you need to be able to understand individual habits. Eventually, I hope that more of these spreadsheets will fall by the wayside, and we will get to a professional solution that is in their system. This will allow us to take some of the man-hours and put more quality into the work, interact with the teams, understand their assumptions, and manage our clients properly. (Top-5 CMO)

The biggest impact that could be made through electronic collaboration is clearly in the areas of inventory management, materials management, quality, and outsourced production management (see Figure 5.9). It is clear that when transactions cross enterprise borders, then the disparity of systems, poorly aligned planning processes, lack of shared forecasting and planning capability, and lack of collaboration across quality review processes are causing the biggest drag on performance.

There is high confidence that if shared process collaboration is coupled with access to precise and timely data by virtual supply teams, the result will be better business performance (see Figure 5.10).

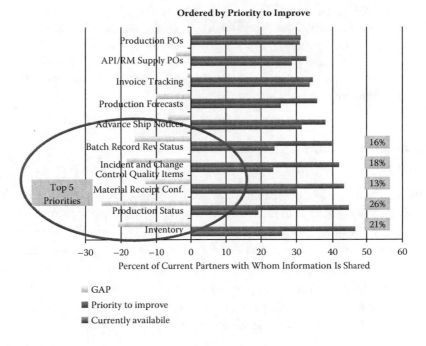

FIGURE 5.9

Some areas (production, inventory, and quality) are the highest priorities to improve and good candidates for collaboration.

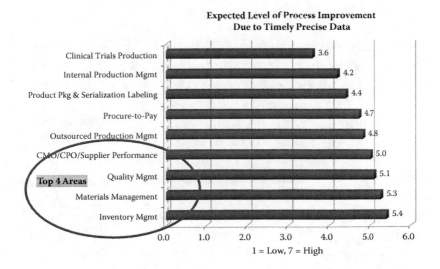

FIGURE 5.10

There is confidence that if supply network teams are able to improve information access and process collaboration, better business performance will result.

> Some CMOs aren't transparent on what caused the delay with a shipment. If we miss production days, they fail to tell us why it happened, and we don't get a good understanding. But if we had a common platform, they would be forced to be more transparent. In some cases, there may be performance indicators that are measured differently, depending on if the starting point is different than yours. (Leading Biophama)

Performance Metrics That Drive Collaboration: What to Measure? How Often?

One of the most important components of collaboration involves establishing a format for regular reviews of key performance indicators (KPIs). KPIs can help identify not only the source of problems, but can drive the source to a root cause that can be addressed through purposive and direct actions. These actions can then be embedded in a new collaborative process that drives not just action based on feedback, but indeed, develops a basis for scenario planning for future issues that have not even occurred yet. As noted by one executive we interviewed:

> We go through performance reviews once a quarter to have face time with customers and review business performance metrics, new projects, and ensure an interdisciplinary format. The best solution to supply chain problems is individuals talking to individuals, and no two relationships with customers are the same. (Top-5 CMO)

The types of KPIs that are monitored will vary for different relationships, but our survey suggests that a basic set of KPIs for certain types of activities provides the basis to solve 80% of the problems that might arise.

For each metric, an important consideration is the relative accuracy (or quality) of information. If information or a KPI is shared and the data isn't accurate, then an unfortunate event is likely to occur. Someone is acting on that information in a manner that will not produce the desired outcome.

The other question that requires consideration is the frequency of updates. That is, how often do the measures need to be updated to provide an appropriate level of change granularity and management oversight?

As shown by the survey results in Figure 5.11, the typical KPIs for major elements are reported on a weekly or monthly basis. No activities were

Production	Monthly	Weekly	Hourly	Accurate/Satisfied?
On-time delivery	×	×		LOW
Order fulfillment accuracy	×	×		LOW
Order fulfillment cycle	×	×		LOW
Materials	**Monthly**	**Weekly**	**Hourly**	**Accurate/Satisfied?**
On-time delivery	×	×		POOR
Avg. material delay	×			VERY POOR
Order fulfillment cycle time	×			VERY POOR
Production/consumption levels	×	×		POOR
Inventory	**Monthly**	**Weekly**	**Hourly**	**Accurate/Satisfied?**
Finished goods	×	×		POOR
API/RM	×	×		VERY POOR
WIP	×	×		VERY POOR
Aging/expiration	×			VERY POOR
Quality	**Monthly**	**Weekly**	**Hourly**	**Accurate/Satisfied?**
On-hold, in-quality, on-order	×	×		VERY POOR
Batch record review (first pass approv)	×	×		VERY POOR
Batch record Review (# of iterations)	×	×		VERY POOR
Change event reviews (% on-time)	×	×		VERY POOR
Deviation event reviews (% recurring)	×	×		VERY POOR
Avg. Closure time	×	×		VERY POOR
Ave # events per batch	×	×		VERY POOR

FIGURE 5.11

KPIs are measured and reported on a relatively infrequent basis and accuracy is poor.

currently reported on a daily or hourly basis. The level of accuracy and satisfaction with these metrics is generally very poor.

Some of the more pressing needs for information and KPIs is in the area of material delays, cycle time, inventory levels in API and work in progress (WIP), information on aging, and lack of visibility into the status of quality reviews. This was particularly problematic for biologics companies, who are keen to be able to see batch records and QP releases to market, in order to determine the status of an order in the system. Pharma companies we spoke with, on the other hand, are more often concerned with product inventory and forecast status.

> We spend a lot of time on batch record status, so a common window really needs to be defined to establish preventive action. For example,

if the customer is doing the QP release to the market, and they have to execute the full batch record, it could sit for three–four weeks before they get to it. We have the product made and sitting, but can't ship it. What if we could track the batch record review and could pull the data electronically? That would present some massive opportunities for efficiencies to be gained. (Leading CMO)

QA [quality assurance] cycle times are a major issue for us. In my opinion, there is a redundancy in review. A CMO's quality system that we have audited and approved is not believed to be good enough. We go through a second review that is often redundant. I have seen some work that one company has done to create scorecards for suppliers based on internal records and internal audits and tracking of batch records. For top suppliers, a quality review isn't needed. (Leading Biotech)

What is most valuable to us is the inventory updates. When are packaging processes completed, what is the accuracy of the data when is it updated in the system, and when is it committed. (Leading Pharma)

A common problem discussed in the interviews is the lack of aligned, defined performance metrics. Managers noted that simple definitions and nomenclature for common metrics such as *on-time* and *batch record release cycle time* were often nonexistent. These comments reflect the lack of a common industry application to drive common performance measures.

There are often misunderstandings regarding what is meant by an on-time delivery. The first promise date is often the customer "wish" date—but we are not able to measure against that. We are able to measure against a promise date based on reasonable cycle times that have been agreed to in a contract. And we can measure in terms of on-time in full. Last year we wanted to be north of 95%, but were between 92% and 94% against promised confirmed date—and our goal is to improve that this year. (Top-5 CMO)

If I need to release a product, I need the batch record. It might take three hours to release it assuming there are no questions. But the supplier wants a three-week lead-time and they don't know when they will get it in—and they ask for this lead time to manage their own scheduling. (Leading Biopharma)

Cost of Poor Visibility to Biopharma

The need for new forms of electronic collaboration is at a peak. Yet many companies have struggled to achieve this, not just because of a lack of systems, but because of a fundamental inability to operationalize the cost of poor performance.

All of the companies recognized that misaligned information, missing data, poor planning, and timeliness of data was a significant cost to the business, but could not quantify the cost of these gaps.

> The main cost of poor information is timeliness and accuracy. Somebody is telling somebody else something, but it is not getting to the right person who needs that information to make a decision. Every link in the supply chain where there is poor information exchange adds the possibility of errors. Maybe that person is in that day or maybe not. And how long does it take before the information reaches them? And meanwhile the clock is ticking on an already inflated lead time. So the only solution to this problem is a big buffer of inventory. (Leading Pharma)

> There are two big issues. One is efficiency—we have people who do nothing but react to situations. Instead of having them plan two, three weeks out, they are always reacting to information. And secondly, we hold more inventory than we would normally need to. We can't quantify the cost of a missed patient dose, or customers who are disgruntled with a lack of execution. The way we manage today, we have a good view of excess and obsolescence because it is an asset than can be expensed, but we don't know the cost of late orders. (Top-5 CMO)

> A good forecast is definitely the key ingredient of solid supply chain activity. If you don't have a forecast that is 93% accurate over an eighteen-month waterfall, you can't plan on what to get into clean rooms, and can't manage all the exceptions that take place. This is especially important on many of the long lead times on many types of materials and glassware. If we could just have an exchange of an eighteen-month forecast, with a six-month frozen horizon—life would be so much easier. We don't even need a formal PO, but just to know that once a forecast hits a window it becomes firm—would make such a massive improvement. (Top-5 CMO)

As shown in the survey responses below, executives and managers believe that improvement in many of the most common supply chain metrics could be improved dramatically through real-time data and multi-enterprise collaboration (see Figure 5.12). Executives expect that the biggest improvements, of 20%–40% over current levels, would be in:

- reduced manual data entry by enabling direct enterprise system-to-system data flows;
- improved agility across supply relationships to respond to variable, global demand;

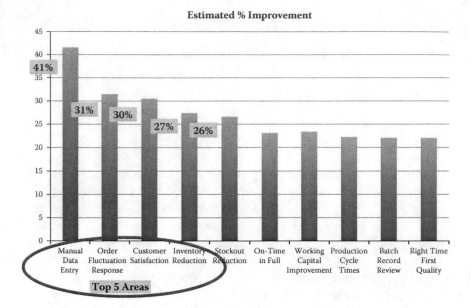

FIGURE 5.12
Expected supply performance gains through access to real-time data and multi-enterprise collaboration are significant.

- decreased finished goods, WIP, and raw material inventory levels; and
- performance on out-of-stock and perfect order (on-time, in-full) metrics.

Significant benefits also lie in several additional business areas including reduced production cycle times, reduced working capital levels, and increased confidence in product quality.

As most executives expected performance improvement across multiple areas of their businesses due to supply collaboration, there is a strong foundation to build a rigorous business case to drive investment.

While the average expected benefit across several measures is significant enough to warrant deeper investigation, if not outright investment by many companies, the opportunities may be even greater in individual cases. According to the survey respondents, many participants are optimistic of achieving substantially greater gains on many metrics.

The pain of *not* having information is clearly the most challenging component (see Figure 5.13). There is a waterfall effect that occurs due to people in the supply chain acting on inaccurate or misleading

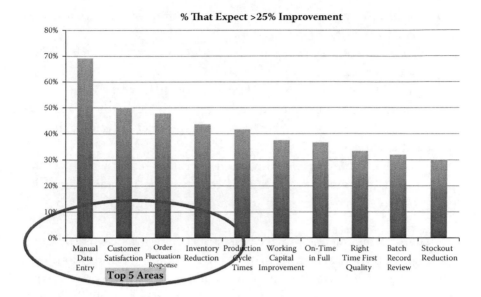

FIGURE 5.13
Many respondents are confident that improvements would exceed 25% over current performance levels on five measures.

information, or the lack of information altogether. As noted by one pharma executive,

> The pain of getting it wrong is that even if we share it, it isn't accurate or correct, and the pain comes from a supplier building more stuff than we really need or holding stock on our behalf. The other pain is obsolescence, and the cost of writing off a stock. There is also the cost of expediting, as well as the time and effort to resolve issues and get to the bottom of what is wrong with the information. The ultimate cost, of course, is the inability to supply customers on time, and a shortage of product. In that situation, it is not just lack of visibility, but a fundamental inability to supply. When things like that go wrong, people look to point fingers and blame others. But the fundamental issue is that there isn't proper sharing of information, and the ways of working aren't allowing people to see the true picture.

If electronic supply network collaboration can help with these issues, what does the solution look like?

Characteristics of a Collaborative Supply Network

The need to drive electronic collaboration requires several components that are important for success.

- **Connectivity:** Connect all companies, facilities, and virtual supply teams across the supply network.
- **Data:** Gain shared access to key production and supply chain data that is accurate and timely.
- **Visibility:** Provide comprehensive yet detailed visibility across all supply relationships and throughout all activities in the production life cycle from order/forecast to final product delivery and into distribution.
- **Collaboration:** Enable joint value creation and better decision making by providing an operational environment for multi-enterprise collaboration on shared business processes in the supply chain.

All of the companies recognized that performance metrics were missing, misaligned, or nonexistent in many of their supply chain relationships. With no good method of tracking and recording transactions and receipts in the supply chain, metrics are not only difficult to define, but difficult to record and monitor.

> There are functional breaches that occur. Once it is distributed into the network, it is lost in transit until we get some confirmation. FedEx may get it there in one day, but it may take another week to get it loaded in. So there is no visibility mechanism that allows you to feel good about that order. We manage by exception, rather than proactively knowing that 98% of our shipments are received. (Leading Pharma)

These results provide an important basis for further discussion with all stakeholders in the life sciences supply network on designing, building, and deploying the operational and technical foundation that provides for true collaboration for the biopharma industry.

6

Maturing the Clinical Trial Supply Chain

One of the key symptoms experienced by clinical trial supply chain organizations is the lack of integrated planning, contract manufacturing, and distribution, resulting in missed deliveries and firefighting on a regular basis. However, these groups are really struggling with a more fundamental root cause, related to understanding key bottlenecks in the process, and where these are occurring. A compendium of issues has created a barrage of diversions, pitfalls, and challenges preventing clinical research teams from making any reasonable headway in establishing standard processes, accurate forecasts, resource plans, or other supply chain planning activities beyond the current mode of firefighting and keeping current clinical operations supplied with product. If this situation continues, it is highly probable that there will be a high level of burnout on the part of individuals in clinical research roles, chronic shortages of material for clinical trials, and more severe business consequences associated with FDA regulatory issues associated with clinical trial reporting and product pipeline approvals.

FINDING: TRIAL COMPLEXITY IS INCREASING

The biggest issues facing clinical supply chain management are threefold: trial design, geographic complexity, and large/small molecule.

1. The complexity of trials is increasing dramatically, in terms of trial design, dose levels, and unscheduled patient visits.
2. There is increasing complexity in geography. Complex trial designs over multiple geographies increases the potential for overages, and

the geographic dispersion leads to an increased probability for things to go awry.

3. There is increasing technical complexity, especially for large molecule and biological materials. These tend to be very high-dollar materials, and the impact of waste is significant.

FINDING: MULTIPLE PERCEPTIONS EXIST IN CLINICAL TEAMS

We begin by summarizing the symptoms identified through my research that involved interviews with clinical teams, as well as insights from supply chain team interviews.

Working capital versus flexibility: One of the common perceptions of clinical managers was that the progress made in reducing working capital and overages had somehow deteriorated clinical supplies availability significantly. This was misleading, as it was also apparent that project teams are behind the efforts to keep costs down, particularly where an expensive comparator is used (e.g., oncology). In one study, the clinical budget holder wanted to reduce cost and cut supply chain overages further without realizing the impact on delivery. In any case, there may be a discrepancy in understanding the drivers behind working capital reduction, as clinical supply is working to help the clinical teams keep their costs down. It may not be clear to some members of the clinical teams where such decisions on overage are being made.

Lack of engagement: Another common theme was the perception that clinical supply was not actively engaged in the early stages of clinical study design because of resource issues. In fact, these resource issues are real, but a good amount of time is also consumed by supply staff in non-value-added activities, including expediting, manual work with spreadsheets, and workload issues.

Lack of flexibility and responsiveness to increasing study complexity: There is also a perception that supply chain teams have become less flexible and able to deal with the increased technical complexity that is arising in many clinical studies.

Need for scenario planning and risk mitigation planning: Clinical research leaders noted that there were problems with the level of preventive risk management at the front end of clinical design that caused problems later during the rollout. Leaders believed that additional support and scenario planning models could provide an important input into clinical study design.

Inadequate systems: A significant problem was the lack of a material resource planning (MRP) system to drive component material planning and release schedules at sites.

Review of clinical trials suggests that a number of problems exist at various stages in the supply chain, as shown in Figure 6.1.

- Unclear roles and responsibilities
- Approvals not aligned with forecasts and material availability
- Label development cycle
- Clinical packaging delays
- Lack of standards tools and plans
- Long lead times
- Internal SM programs not developed
- Vendor performance
- Inadequate capacity
- Shipping temperature excursions
- Low data integrity

While these issues are perhaps viewed as *nothing catastrophic* in the short-term, there is a lot of stress for trial managers. In many cases, however, such minor issues can delay clinical trials, and in a worst-case scenario, lose market share if the drug is late to market.

These issues raise the broader issue of how to create a sustainable and resilient supply chain. Whether you're at the beginning or the middle of your supply chain improvement efforts, the question you must always confront at each new milestone is: What next step can we take that will most effectively move the process forward? Or, in tough years with slim budgets: What's the one thing we can do to best keep from losing our momentum entirely? This is a key foundational assumption for how an organization must begin to consider the clinical trials process.

The Supply Chain Maturity (SCM) Assessment Model was designed to guide organizations on these next steps, whether you are trying to incrementally improve processes within planning, sourcing, manufacturing, delivery, or return logistics.

Given the current culture and need to drive change in biopharma cultures, the development of a maturity model with formal surveys and interviews is

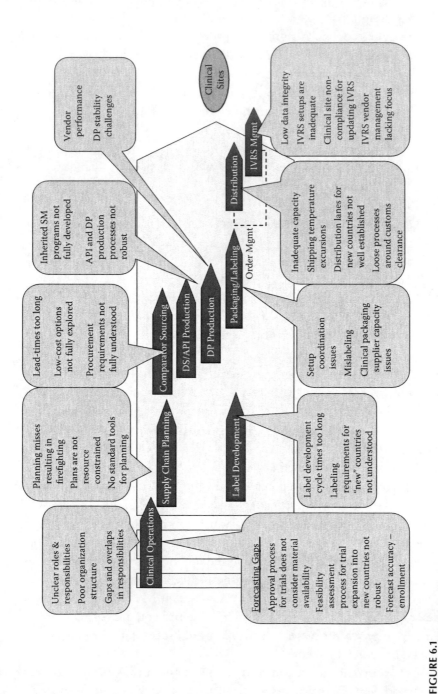

FIGURE 6.1
Typical challenges exist across the clinical supply chain.

important in being able to "level-set" the organization, establish a common view of the current state, and identify a desired future state.

There exists significant diversity in current business processes, and there is a need to identify where the critical gaps are, explore existing best practices, and target key areas for improvement or leveraging of best practices.

Developing a full-scale maturity model is not as important as identifying the areas to be benchmarked, and then collecting fair observations.

CONCEPT OF SCM MATURITY

According to our model, clinical trials supply chain management maturity occurs as organizations move through five stages, ultimately reaching an end goal of having a completely extended organization with full integration of activities between companies, their customers, and their trading partners. Each successive step includes more functions and more firms within a given supply chain.

What a company does at each step and *how* it does it are equally important. If it performs regular sales forecasts based on historical data and mathematical models, it is just as important that the company employs this data in a collaborative fashion, providing it to key groups both inside and outside the company.

The five stages of maturity describe the progression of activities toward effective clinical supply chain integration. These stages are based on the maturity framework described earlier in Chapters 1 and 2 of this book.

Clinical Trials Supply Chain Core Processes

Supply chains can be assessed using the Supply Chain Operations Reference (SCOR®) model framework to benchmark SCM best practice usage across industries (Figure 6.2). In a similar manner, the SCOR model can be applied to clinical trial supply chains, using a modified application framework. This model is intentionally holistic, and includes suppliers and *their* suppliers as well as customers and *their* customers. The model focuses on the four key process areas: plan, source, make, and deliver. (Return is relevant in the clinical trial setting.) Enablers, supporting processes and infrastructure,

The SCOR Structure

The boundaries of any model must be well defined

FIGURE 6.2
The SCOR structure source, http://supply-chain.org/scor

such as information technology, are also included in the model and in the core process assessment survey. These elements correspond to the following core processes in the clinical supply chain:

- **Plan:** Clinical planning activities
- **Source:** Negotiations, contracting, and relationship management with key clinical suppliers (contract manufacturers [CMs], warehouses depots, interactive voice response system [IVRS] vendors, third-party logistics providers, etc.)
- **Make:** Management of clinical CMs (Active Pharmaceutical Ingredient [API], fill and finish, label and pack)
- **Deliver:** Clinical logistics and global distribution

The mapping of these elements to processes is shown in Figure 6.3. In this figure, the dotted line represents the essential departure point between demand (clinical trials team patient forecasts) and supply (actual production of placebos, comparators, and product with appropriate packaging and blind labeling for country distribution).

SCM best practice usage within this framework is measured and described using the following five-item Likert scale measuring the frequency or institutionalization of the principle or practice:

1: Never or does not exist
2: Sometimes

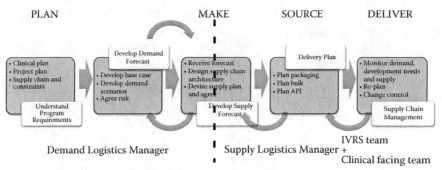

FIGURE 6.3
Demand and supply management in clinical trials.

3: Frequently
4: Mostly
5: Always or definitely exists
NA: Not applicable or don't know

The higher the number, the more institutionalized the practice, which reflects process maturity and reliability. Benchmarking scores are summed and organized by SCOR model category and SCM maturity components and compared to the database mean.

Results

Overall Maturity

The mean for the overall supply chain for clinical trials in our study is between a defined and measured level (Figure 6.4), and is below the industry mean in terms of process documentation, organizational structure, and performance measures. Although basic SCM processes are defined and documented, they are not always being followed. The order commitment, planning, and distribution processes, for example, are available in flow charts, and changes to these processes must now go through a formal procedure. Jobs and organizational structures include an SCM aspect, but remain basically traditional.

It is interesting to note that overall, many individuals in clinical supply organizations are very process focused. This is perhaps explainable by the fact that many of the individuals in these companies come from

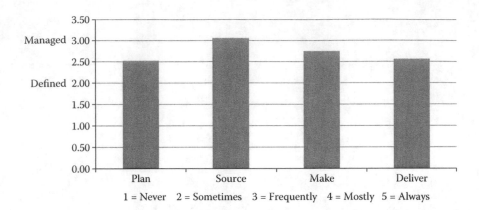

1 = Never 2 = Sometimes 3 = Frequently 4 = Mostly 5 = Always

FIGURE 6.4

Clinical supply chain operating at a Defined to Managed level.

a biotech or chemistry background, both of which are highly process-focused industries. The biggest gap here is in organization structure, which is not particularly process focused, and appears to lag somewhat. The lack of meaningful performance measures and organizational process structure reflects the fact that organizational roles and responsibilities are not well defined and understood, and that the lack of metrics makes management and control of processes all the more challenging.

Individuals interviewed emphasized that firefighting is the norm. This is a primary symptom of processes that are unstable and unreliable. As one individual noted, "We react to emergencies well and we are extremely proficient at crisis management." Another notable theme was the expressed need for improved planning capabilities. Lean systems are characterized by stable production and low inventory in the system. Compare this state to the following observation:

We need to begin creating safety stock levels, rational order points, designing our business around service levels, which require more than just making it to the 100% level, but rather include some aspect of unforecasted demand. Inventory can forgive a lot of sins in the manufacturing world, but it is the price of a hedge that should be gladly paid to avoid disruption to the clinical operations world. We should build inventory until we improve processes to the point that we can demonstrate that we can routinely supply our clinical programs without interruption or crisis management.

In the remainder of this report, we review maturity assessments for each of the core supply chain processes of plan, source, make, and deliver.

Plan: Clinical Supply Chain Planning

Our assessment of one clinical trials planning process in biopharmaceutical companies we surveyed is between level 2 (leveraged) and 3 (managed). Planning is the critical lynchpin that binds the different elements of the clinical supply chain (clinical ops, contract manufacturing, and logistics) together. Effective planning ensures that coordination among these groups is occurring, and that changes in plans are acted on in an appropriate time frame. Planning success is a function of obtaining reasonably accurate forecasts from clinical operations, feeding these into standardized planning processes, and regular communication of plans and dialogue with clinical operations and stakeholders on supply chain capabilities and limitations (see Figure 6.5). Planners must then make trade-offs on supply and demand that will ensure that high-priority clinics and programs are getting their kits and products when needed. In the process, sacrifices may need to be made, as some programs will have to be delayed or compromised if there are limitations to capacity. (Note: In this table, "industry mean" refers to non-biopharma companies.)

On the demand side, there will always be gaps due to changes in clinical operations, patient recruiting patterns, and changes in programs. Similarly, on the supply side, unpredictable events in global logistics and quality issues at contract manufacturing sites will drive variation in supply side processes. However, there is mounting evidence, as shown in this assessment, that parts of the planning process are not working effectively to align supply and demand. All of the measures in the maturity assessment were significantly below the industry mean, with the exception of formal meetings occurring within the right time frame. Although these meetings are indeed occurring, it is apparent that planning outcomes and effective communication updates are still not happening in a predictable manner. As shown in Figure 6.5, the areas that are rated as weak in the planning process are largely in three primary areas: (1) forecast accuracy, (2) lack of metrics, and (3) lack of standardized processes. It is worthwhile to look at these areas in greater detail.

Forecast Accuracy

It is clear that clinical trial planners who are planning new trials do not have a robust forecasting process, and that if there is a process, it is not being followed. This is to be expected, since most clinical trial design

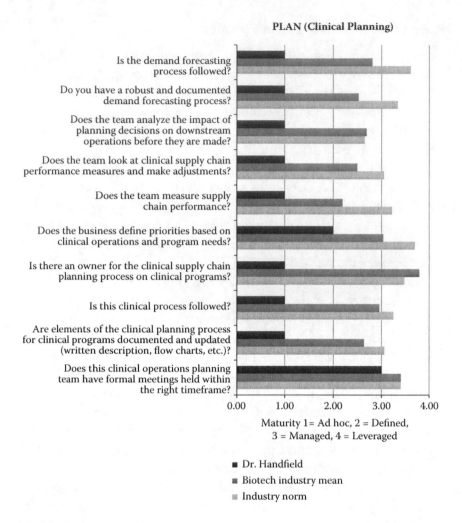

FIGURE 6.5
Clinical planning.

teams are not operationally focused; think in terms of patients, not product units; and often have no idea what happens or what is required once a trial is launched. Although the score measuring whether forecasts use historical country recruiting in an appropriate time frame rated 2.80, these were still well below the industry means. The biggest problem is the fact that forecast accuracy is not measured or acted on, and that the forecasts are not being used to make adjustments to CM or logistics depot plans, and if they are, they are not occurring in a timely manner. More specifically, individuals emphasized that it was not so much the accuracy of the forecasts that was the problem, but the inability of clinical operations to provide forecasts aligned with planning lead-time horizons. This theme was echoed in several of the interviews with clinical trials managers we conducted in this study.

> We need to have forecasts for a trial that is starting in a year, but they (the clinical team) can't tell us the dosage. The enrollment forecasts are never accurate, and we have no indication on where in the world patients will show up. They will give us a list of countries where they are going and where the patients are, but then change it based on what they believe is a legitimate forecast for demand. And if they change it, then it becomes very difficult to get an import license for some countries.

> I would really like to work on creating a better forecast. The clinical program team meetings are important, but we always feel like we are reading between the lines of what they are saying. Are their plans really slipping, are they really realistic? Thirty to 40% of my time is spent in various meetings, and there is a lot of following up. When you have a slip all of a sudden, then you are managing a crisis. You start with a plan, and then you have a slip, and now you're reacting. No amount of Plan B contingency will help. It is not always due to the clinical forecast, but more due to execution failure—a batch wasn't manufactured on time, things were not delivered on time, or issues with delivery or quality.

> What we get from clinical ops in terms of the demand picture is never firm, and the reliability of their plans is always in question. We have been exposed to that time and time again. Let's get a complete demand picture and we promise to manage to that. The current scheme of having spreadsheets everywhere, and trying to determine which spreadsheet is the most current one, is absolute madness. As a planner, if patient enrollment changes within less than the planner lead time, we cannot react to those changes. It takes us seven and a half months to manufacture our own drug. It takes six weeks or longer to ship to Russia. If we could only get a picture on where we are in terms of cumulative demand, and have that come out of a planning meeting, things would get much better.

> Their Contract Research Organization (CROs) give them a forecast on the last week of the month, which is an input they put into the clinical trial management system (CTMS). We have told them that if you have a system of record to which all reports are given, that should drive our planning on the demand handshake. But it turns out that they (clinical ops) aren't focused on maintaining the integrity of that system. So I asked CTM to give me a CRO forecast, as well as an optimistic version, because I don't

want to be caught, but don't want to artificially increase my overages either. But that is tough for them to do.

We have a planning tool that is capable of processing scenarios in demand and how supply plans align with demand plans. Now that we have that capability, we can enter a single record of the forecast, and go to conservative or optimistic scenarios, and quickly assess if we need to refine our supply times. And every two weeks we can see if things have changed over that lead time, review it, and adjust. But to make this work, an official handoff of demand needs to happen. A single forecast should occur at the clinical design team level. This has to be a single, official forecast—don't give me a spreadsheet that changes all the time. This is a behavioral change that has to happen in the design of clinical trials.

Lack of Metrics

The lack of clear metrics to manage clinical supply and demand is problematic in many organizational clinical supply chain teams. Metrics are lacking in a number of areas, including forecast accuracy, supply chain performance, and ability to have visibility into events, and adjust to drop-in orders or disruptions in the contract manufacturing or logistics environment. This is equivalent to driving a car without a speedometer, odometer, or gas indicator. Some of the comments from supply chain managers are shown below:

Our biggest opportunity for improvement is if we could begin creating safety stock levels, rational order points, and designing our business around service levels. This requires more than just making to the 100% level, but rather including some aspect of unforecasted demand.

We need better information from clinical early and more visibility into ongoing activities, especially logistics.

We need to implement IT solutions for clinical supply management and visibility holistically. We also need to establish our capacity, and resource all of our clinical supply chain departments (full-time [employees], or FTEs) to reasonably manage workload.

It would be great if we could build a financial outlook on packaging runs, and build a strategy on optimal number of packaging jobs for a study. We could run scenarios on whether we manage it by one run a quarter, holding the quantity constant, or holding it constant and changing the timing. But we don't have the opportunity to influence cost, because we have no visibility, no metrics, and so right now all we can do is manage supply and demand and not improve cost.

We have a manufacturing process, but very little measurement of it. Our metrics on clinical operations are weak. If we have any metrics, we don't analyze them, or extract meaningful information from them. We don't look at why deviation rates are going up, or whether they are in control. We are successful purely through brute force and cannot justify whether it's working or not. If I were the boss, I would ask this group to prove to me what their nominal capacity is, and then address resource issues based on that.

Lack of Standard Processes

When planning processes are not standardized, they evolve into essentially a firefighting activity. Numerous comments reflect the fact that planning is able to "respond to critical issues and drive to resolution, keeping patients in mind in our efforts to supply sites with drug." They also noted, "We are very good at executing last-minute changes. So even if we have less than the original lead time, we make sure it will be done in time anyhow." Although firefighting was viewed as a "strength" of many supply chain planning teams, many wish it was not the case. This is largely due to the fact that planning roles and responsibilities are not aligned with other groups such as quality assurance (QA), logistics, and clinical operations. A formal tactical planning meeting with clear charters and roles could improve this process.

We have clear plans on what needs to be done and when, from a demand standpoint. But the clinical people don't live in our world. We can construct clear plans on what to make and when to make it, but the lead times are long. We only receive production plans on a monthly basis, but it is a red herring. The real issue is in how we conduct clear handoffs in the supply chain. If we are at a level 2 today, the only way we get to level 3 is to map out processes, understand what it takes to get drug product to the clinic, and define who is responsible for what piece, and clearly delineate roles and responsibilities. Sales and operations planning is not the issue. We have those forums, and communication is going to help that, but lack of communication addresses only 10% to 20% of the issues. The others are related to tactical handoffs and inadequate information provided on a timely basis within the right lead times.

Communications between clinical teams and supply chain is an issue. Multiple times we have to explain and reexplain our constraints to them, and they can't understand why we have these long timelines. They think we're padding these lead times on purpose. And if we have to spend an hour on the phone every time explaining things to a clinical manager and communicating effectively, it sucks up our time and things get held up.

Very often, no one knows details regarding global regulatory issues in logistics, but planning is expected to know these things. And we get questions about things we don't know anything about, including regulatory issues, etc., because logistics has the execution and these issues get pushed back to us. And so if we don't know, we are accused of not doing anything.

If planning is at a level 2, the single biggest action that can drive it to level 3, as noted by this assessment, is mapping of core processes, and designation of clear roles and responsibilities among clinical ops, planning, logistics, and contract manufacturing. Measures and visibility into events that will permit management of unplanned drop-in orders will increase the capability of this group immeasurably, and will also reduce the amount of firefighting and crisis management that characterizes this group.

Source: Relationship Management with Key Clinical Suppliers

Relative to the other processes, sourcing processes are relatively well developed in many clinical supply chain teams. For example, there is a high score relative to supplier collaboration in developing planning. Discussions with executives reveal that contract manufacturing managers have established true collaborative relationships with key suppliers. In many cases these suppliers are providing excellent results in terms of continuous improvement, temperature deviation problems, capacity planning, and responsiveness. However, as indicated in Chapter 3, many CMOs [care management organizations] are still reliant on largely manual planning and order sharing processes, which are subject to a lot of error. Indeed, many of the comments we received noted that strategic relationships were managed well, and that sourcing risk had been reduced through avoiding single sources in critical situations. They also felt that precontract RFI/RFQ processes, as well as postcontract supplier management processes were working effectively. Overall, the decision processes were believed to be operating at a managed (3) level of maturity.

In terms of weaknesses in sourcing processes, the biggest gap was in the area of procure-to-pay approvals and processes. Many individuals interviewed expressed continued frustration with the many challenges associated with having a simple invoice approved, and the length of time required to do so. A lead contract manufacturing director noted:

The bulk of my time (60%–80%) is spent executing the internal sourcing approvals. If we have a campaign, and I want to make product, getting our internal procurement and finance people to agree to it is the most difficult part. PO [purchase order] signing alone can take over a month, just to order materials. In the quoting process, we meet with the vendor, and negotiation with the CMOs is *not* the problem. We tell them, they do it in the agreed-upon time, but we continue to be our own worst nightmare. We have confounding internal processes, and a lack of framework or direction on who approves what. It is extremely difficult to get work done and conduct business with our CMOs as a result.

If I had one wish, it would be to have a single source and venue for planning what we make and agree to buy, and then cut people loose to do that work, and not fight the PO approvals, the budgeting, etc. Let's get the bulk plan, and define what we have to do now to get ready for shipment. It is ready, and gives it the green light. Today, I am dying a death by 1,000 cuts. I have to show a quality agreement, master supply agreement, original quote from vendor, contract summary sheet showing that I had review from quality and regulatory and development chemist, and a PO request sheet and manufacturing plan that shows why we need this, and then have to get a letter from development that is a narrative of why we need to make this product. And then we have to buy those hours on the plan, and eventually it is approved.

Another issue raised is the lack of coordination that often occurs between sourcing professionals and other groups in the company (see Figure 6.6). For instance, one individual noted, "We need to continue to define the role of sourcing in existing vendor performance evaluation. Is this a role of sourcing, or of contract manufacturing?" This lack of coordination also included potential worries that suppliers were bearing the brunt of Biogen's internal struggles: "How do we keep a solid schedule and setting up our suppliers for success? I feel our internal problems often 'bleed' onto our suppliers." There were also some questions regarding the interaction between different groups, resulting in suboptimal decisions. For instance, one individual emphasized, "We need to look at the process in a more holistic way and make improvements in the process that will streamline the daily operations (i.e., currently we purchase comparators and package and label them, why can't the comparators be purchased locally and avoid the operation completely?)."

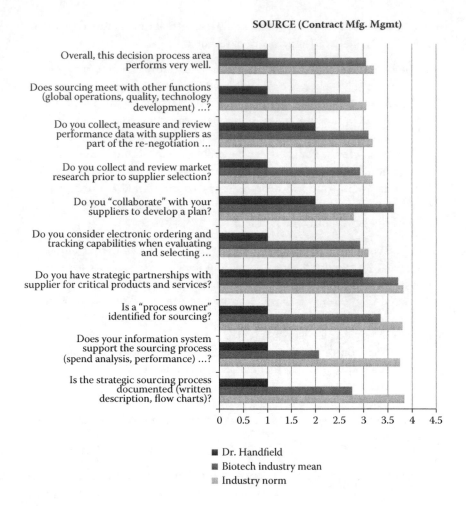

FIGURE 6.6
Clinical trials sourcing.

Make: Management of Clinical Contract Manufacturers (API, Fill and Finish, Label and Pack)

Processes in the *make* area were also better than the norm in a number of areas, based on assessments made by associates. For example, teams scored significantly higher than the industry norm in areas such as ownership and management of the relationship with CMs by contract manufacturing management, and sharing of updated planning and scheduling information with suppliers. There was also recognition that supplier lead times are a major consideration in the planning process. There appears to be relatively good dialogue between contract manufacturing and their suppliers, with updated lead times, effective weekly planning meetings, and sharing of information. Several individuals we spoke with emphasized that they had defined a high level of trust and collaboration with their key suppliers through frequency and content of communication, regular performance reviews, and informal dialogues and continuous improvement efforts. However, the overall level of performance for this area was 2.75, indicating a level between Defined and Managed as before.

The overall score was brought down by several glaring weaknesses identified by individuals in the survey. The most important of these and the greatest weakness was the ability to escalate changes in production through a formal documented approval process. Because there is a lack of a formal documented process to deal with sudden slips and changes in scheduling CMs, people are discovering the problems of an informal process that uses workarounds to meet sudden deadline changes:

> I have a real talent gap. I thought I would need only technical people who could work with us and solve problems. But what I found was that the most successful people I had were not the technocrats, but those that have a developed social network within the company, who have placed markers with favors that they have done with people, and can do a quick follow-up with people who will take their call. What I need are relationship managers—you need people who are good at contacting and negotiating with decision makers, making them feel good, working around the process, and knowing how to make things happen. I would certainly like to be at a point where I manage a schedule and deal with issues as they come up, but what I've discovered is I need people who have a network of people they can go to. Because there is no process and no formal network, we have to work through an informal social network. This is an outcome of what the design of our supply chain organization has created—an environment where we make it so difficult to get things made, including specifications, authorization to manufacture, and approvals at every step.

Related to this issue was the inability to buffer these deviations with appropriate levels of API inventory to manage inaccurate forecasts. This was being blamed, by and large, on the planning group, with an acknowledgment that overproduction of API was unacceptable yet was causing major delays in clinical trials (see Figure 6.7).

> Our clinical planning group separates demand management between Good Manufacturing Practices (GMP) and non-GMP demand. When they

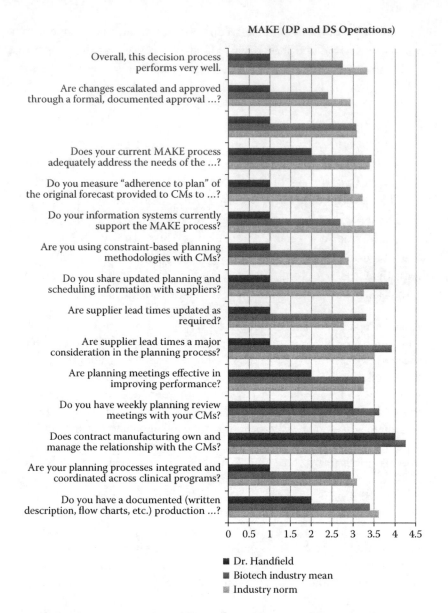

FIGURE 6.7
Clinical trials production.

plan for API, they only place orders for API to make requisite dosage form for clinics. But, they don't plan for extra API for contingencies, emergencies, process loss, yield loss, cosmetic rejects for samples, or other things that occur on a regular basis. They only order the exact amount required for the dose. Manufacturing tries to add overage, but not a lot. But then we still end up short, all because we don't want to throw material away. But what is the cost of *not* having it? By amalgamating GMP and non-GMP, we are *shorting* material for development, and if we don't develop the dosage forms now, then next year the trial will be delayed. We live hand to mouth in API and all other downstream activities, all because we don't want to throw it away. I don't know why that is an issue. If you want to hit the bottom line, and this is a risky business, then should you be sensitive to write-offs? We are measuring the distance to a moon with a ruler—we might waste a few grams of API now, or pay a million dollars later to avoid delaying the trial.

If we can get a 10-kilo molecule from research into development, we have a good shot at getting a formulation done. But getting someone to buy that even though we don't know what the dosage will be, is what is needed. We need to have some stomach for overage and obsolescence in Phase 1 or 2, to avoid the cost of delaying a trail.

The second piece that was lacking was the effective information systems to improve planning with key contract manufacturers. This was noted by several managers who expressed their frustration with current CM planning systems.

We have a couple of different systems to model demand versus supply. The current system is a very good system, but it is very, very focused on entering patient enrollment projections and site rollout projections—and if supply meets demand or not. And we also have a very big database to input every manufacturing activity. But what we need is to somehow integrate these two systems, so that if you input a lot into the database it would populate our clinical planning system.

A final piece of the puzzle relates to the ability to manage quality, which is also dramatically understaffed. Managers noted that QA was a major problem in managing contract manufacturing processes.

In my role, I am not empowered to make quality decisions, and I cannot weigh in. Every QA decision requires sign-off or approval from someone in QA. Getting them to get to a consensus is tough, and as a result I spend a lot of time trying to coax an answer out of them. We could have a whole discussion on how it is set up, but ultimately no matter what happens, most QA sign-offs are routine made by two people in the organization. So why is that a problem? Because those two people are in Denmark. Why can't associates be empowered to make a decision? We have an in-process check, and can QA make a decision right now?

In every case, they give the same answer: no, have to take it back to disposition and there is a backlog of decision making.

Deliver: Clinical Logistics and Global Distribution

Perhaps the biggest and most glaring weakness in current clinical supply chains is in the area of global logistics and distribution. Overall, clinical logistics rated as a 2.5, between Defined and Managed, but scores were particularly weak in a number of areas. Many of these stem from the lack of a rigorous documented logistics process and the subsequent inability to say "no" to last-minute changes. Logistics is effectively promising to deliver when they have no basis on which to make the promise, and no means to push back on requirements. Because logistics is at the tail end of the supply chain, it is often absorbing the impacts of delays, changes, inaccurate forecasts, drop-in orders, etc. Further, the systems and metrics prevent logistics from tracking orders into clinics, nor can they measure inventory levels in the chain. Because they are driving blind (no out-of-stock measures, no clinical customer order delivery measures, and no visibility to order status), the ability of this function to deal with the complexities of a global logistics and distribution network is challenged.

> Our problems are too numerous to outline, but here are a few of the biggest issues. Communication as a whole needs to be improved significantly. There is a lack of defined procedures in the clinical world. Roles and responsibilities are assumed on a case-by-case basis. There is no capability to track and confirm inventory, and no visibility anywhere in the system. Information systems for CROs, our planning system, and different transportation providers also exist in isolation from one another. Logistics analysts literally have to dig up a tracking number and look at a carrier's website to track it. Due to the workload in logistics, there is a lack of follow-up and closure on shipments; they could be stuck in customs, but there is no capability for follow-up. Different item codes exist in the IVRS, and as well as in our CRO's packaging system.

Another major challenge is the fact that this area is dramatically under-resourced, with little formal process documentation outlining roles and responsibilities. This was noted in detail by several managers:

> Planning is a problem, and I believe there is a real dearth of capability in that group, in terms of staffing, oversight, and familiarity with the process.

We need to find individuals who are familiar with manufacturing, regulatory processes, etc. Logistics does *not* have the right skills, in terms of import logistics, setting up a depot, ensuring local customers and various countries are compensated. It is really hard if you haven't done it before, and their people are making mistakes along the way in the clinical application, import licenses, what is put forth, arranging for in-country distributors, etc.

We don't have enough logistics analysts and planners assigned to cover the multiple clinical programs. There is clearly a lack of ownership and coverage associated with these individuals, leading to severe problems with workflow coverage. I estimate that a logistics analyst could probably cover, at a maximum, five programs depending on size and complexity, (versus the current coverage of sixteen). However, additional capacity planning is required to verify and validate this estimate. There is a lack of accountability for backup staff when someone is on vacation, etc.

The interface with IVRS systems was also identified as a critical problem that was effectively limiting many companies' ability to replenish clinics. However, this is often pushed to the back burner, due to the number of "hot" items coming into the logistics group on a regular basis (see Figure 6.8).

We have a hot item coming in every hour (at least eight per day on average). We need to follow up and work on these issues. If we had more time, we could spend time on avoiding these issues. For instance, we need to be able to set up IVRS systems to support the trigger of new orders, loading the product to the IVRS so that product will be shipped, setting up protocols with distribution partners, telling them how to handle our product, communicating shipping requirements and documents to sign, review, and ship. The problem is that you have different documentation, labels, and protocols in every country that we go into. And we have limited knowledge of IVRS systems, and it is not clear who is responsible for backups, and there is no accountability. We know that we are supposed to be responsible, but we can't handle it.

We have no training plan, no procedures, and yet one person may be managing five programs. We need not just resources, but SOPs [standard operating procedures], and defined roles and responsibilities. For instance, we have someone who is two weeks into our group, and the only way we train her is by sitting with us, because we have no formal documentation, no process flow diagrams, etc.

We really need some sort of IT solution for gaining clinical material visibility at distribution centers/depots and in transit. Further, we need

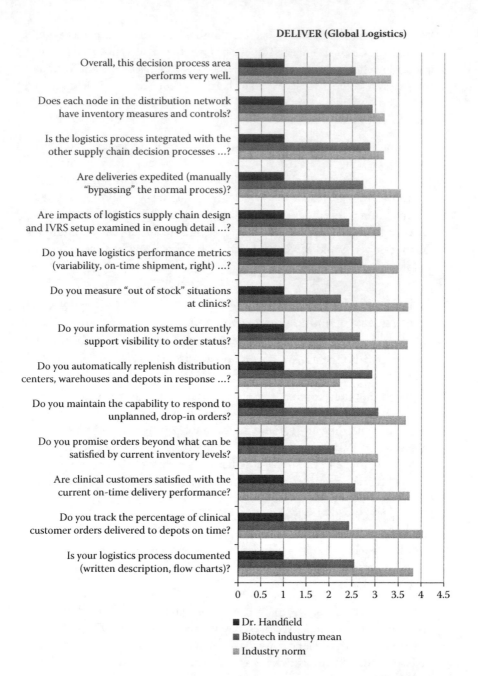

FIGURE 6.8
Logistics.

clarification of roles and responsibilities at touch points with other supply chain groups. Finally, we need to think about resourcing the group appropriately with full time FTEs to manage the workload.

CONCLUSIONS AND RECOMMENDATIONS

All of the employees at companies I interviewed had strong dedicated people working in the clinical operations supply chain. These individuals have pride in their work, and have a deep commitment and concern for patients and ensuring that they will get their products as needed. Unfortunately, many clinical supply chains are not functioning as they should.

Some of the direct quotes from interviews are summarized below:

- Supply chains have a maturity between level 2 (Defined) and level 3 (Managed) maturity (pockets of advanced practices exist, but are not consistently deployed).
- Companies need to shore up the SCM foundation and build a broad, stable level 3 maturity in order to achieve their goals of increasing perfect orders. Critical gaps exist in planning processes, sourcing, contract manufacturing, and sourcing processes.
- Moving toward a last-patient-in planning state can improve coordination and allow prioritization of supply chain planning and execution processes. Clear definition of roles and responsibilities and a documented current state versus future state map will address many of the current challenges that exist.
- Without a significant effort to stabilize current processes, there is a high probability that the problems that exist today will escalate, especially in the face of increased numbers of clinical programs in many biopharmaceutical companies. There is no second-place trophy in this case.

To drive improvement in core supply chain processes to a level 3 maturity (Managed), biopharmaceutical companies will need to do the following:

- **Define planning roles and responsibilities with clinical operations:** Significant opportunities for collaboration and joint planning with strategic contract manufacturers as well as clinical operations should be exploited to drive these initiatives. Specifically, the application of a regularly scheduled tactical forecasting and planning meeting to update clinical trials information, to ensure alignment between planning, contract manufacturing, and logistics, will be a critical step to ensure a firm handoff between clinical and planning groups, and can serve as a forum in which to identify changes that will impact the supply chain. This needs to become a discipline that is driven by metrics and changes in behaviors, with consequences for lack of compliance with the planning process.

- **Improve the sourcing approval process:** Significant delays exist today in the way that manufacturing contracts are approved. These delays are due to excessive controls that exist in procure-to-pay approval processes, which are not necessarily improving control over cost. To improve this process, the entire procure-to-pay process should be process mapped, with legal, finance, and procurement stakeholders engaged to ensure fiduciary controls are met, but not at the expense of excessive paperwork, signatories, or wait times.

- **Improve coordination between contract manufacturing, quality assurance, and API planning:** Although relationship management processes between companies and key contract manufacturers are exceptional in terms of maturity, the inability of contract manufacturing personnel to effectively coordinate internally with other groups is hampered by a lack of communication, lack of tools, and resource limitations within the QA group. Coordination is occurring today through informal social networks, because formal coordination is broken or does not exist. This is not sustainable in an environment where volumes are escalating and resources are constrained. Clinical supply chain teams are often further constrained, API batch sizes designated by planning are not optimized against the cost of multiple smaller batches and the hidden cost of delaying trials nine months in the future. To remedy these issues, value stream mapping of current drug products (DP) and drug substance (DS) processes should occur, as well as the development of formal channels for communication. Further, resource gaps in contract manufacturing, quality assurance, and process requirements need to be assessed to address the most glaring deficiencies that exist.

- **Design and build a logistics tracking and planning system that leverages an IVRS:** Many logistics processes are no doubt the biggest weakness that exists in the supply chain. The function has limited visibility into inventory or in-transit shipments, few metrics on stock-outs or on-time delivery, and a dearth of capability. Global logistics is a complex field that requires detailed knowledge of rapidly changing legal and customs documents, how to set up depots in a new country, obtaining import licenses, etc. Further, the issue of temperature deviations cannot be solved by one new resource that is brought in, as this is a process issue that spans multiple suppliers and logistics providers, and is very complex in nature. These capabilities are not resident in the individuals who work in logistics, and even if they were, individuals here are too busy "babysitting" shipments that are in the pipeline. A complete overhaul of the logistics process is required, but in the short term, this may require bringing in external resources to stabilize the system and ensure that current programs are not off-track.

- **Create a competency map and career path for clinical supply chain positions:** There are glaring gaps in talent and capabilities that exist across all areas of the current supply chain. In addition, individuals who do possess advanced skills and competencies are often under-utilized and relegated to firefighting and execution activities. A comprehensive skills and talent assessment, along with a career planning process, could serve to attract talented individuals into supply chain and lead to improved technical and planning capabilities, so that there is less reliance on QA and other functions.

If deployed, we project that the benefits to organizations that improve to a level 3 or level 4 are estimated to be as follows:

- Decrease program to clinic lead times by 30%–40%.
- Improve perfect order percentage to clinics by 40%–50%.
- Decrease stock-out events by 20%–30%.
- Reduce cost of expired material by 20%.
- Reduce PO approval times by 40%–50%.

However, the most significant benefit to be achieved by reaching stabilization at level 3 maturity is the ability to bring products to clinics on time as promised, and be first to market with innovative biomedical technologies that will save and improve lives.

7

Blueprint for the Future

The passing of the Obama Healthcare Reform Act, and the subsequent vote by the Supreme Court on the requirement that forces individuals to pay a tax if they do not comply, is perhaps not as surprising as the press would have you believe. As I've noted in many of my blogs (http://scm.ncsu.edu/blog), "Obamacare is simply a symptom of the much deeper problems that underlie the healthcare industry." In fact, the much more concerning "drop-dead" date (October 1, 2012). Today, Medicare in the national hospital value-based purchasing (VBP) program has mandated by the Patient Protection and Affordable Care Act (PPACA). A VBP score is calculated based on the quality of outcomes. Recently, a national analysis of hospital performance by VHA Inc. calculated a national median VBP score of 53, when hospitals likely will need scores higher than 70 to maximize their Medicare reimbursements. The median risk for VBP loss is $250,000 for 2012 for hospitals, and $1.88 million over five years. To avoid these losses, the biggest cost savings in future reimbursement models comes from keeping patients out of hospitals, which in turn reduces hospital revenues; this is an incredible paradox. Today we are stuck with a siloed and fragmented system, and uncoordinated care. A recent study found that 13% of patients sixty or older had to have tests redone, 36% received conflicting information, and 76% left a physician's office or hospital confused about what to do next in their care.

By 2017, $857 billion of healthcare spending will be under the new Healthcare Reform Act provisions.[*] To complicate matters, 96% of spending in 2017 will be on patients with four or more chronic conditions who may be seeing as many as five to eleven different physicians. So accountable care organizations (ACOs) are designed to try to reduce the number

---

[*] United States Congressional Record. http://thomas.loc.gov/cgi-bin/query/z?r113:S28JA3-0015

of duplicated services, mitigate the high cost of out-of-network providers, better transition strategies, and provide better information sharing. From a financial perspective, the mix of private to government healthcare spending is approximately at a 50/50 split, but by 2030, 75% of a hospital's payer mix will be Medicare or Medicaid, which is a recipe for bankruptcy of the economy.

The challenges facing providers in the years between 2014 and 2020 massive, so complex, and so forbidding, yet executives in this industry are pretty much *inert*. That is the best description for the state of the industry as I have been able to discern based on my interactions with industry executives over the past four years.

It is clear that there are going to be some tough choices to make in healthcare, regardless of politics. The ACO discussion to date has been limited to high-flying ideals of bureaucrats, who come up with vague terms such as *clinical integration, meaningful use of information technology, evidence-based medicine*, and *cost efficiency*, yet provide no formal methods for determining how to deploy these measures. In the 429-page document developed by the Centers for Medicare and Medicaid Services (CMS), ACOs are organizations whose primary care providers are accountable for coordinating care for at least 5,000 Medicare beneficiaries, as a separate legal entity. These organizations must provide better care for individuals, better health for populations based on preventive services, and lower growth in expenditures, a great concept called *patient-centeredness*.

A big chunk of Medicare reimbursement is tied to something called *comparative effectiveness*. This means that there must be a firmer scientific basis for determining the clinical value and cost–benefit of devices, drugs, and interventions through comparative effectiveness research (CER). This is intended to avoid using technologies that are adopted into practice without sufficient evidence and that caused harm to patients, including high-dose chemotherapy, drugs like Vioxx, and bone morphogenetic protein, which has a risk of sterility in men.

All of this comes together in the fact that ACOs are required to implement evidence-based medicine. This means that hospitals are to be held accountable not only for the cost of the care they provide, but for the cost of services performed by doctors and other health care providers in the thirty days after a Medicare patient leaves the hospital.

The other issue that complicates things concerns bundled payments. Under this format, a provider is no longer paid in terms of a fee for service while a patient is in the hospital. In a fee-for-service model, each member of the medical team—the radiologist, the cardiologist, the anesthesiologist, and perhaps the consulting physician who works with the patient afterward—is paid separately based on their activity. In bundled payments, a single fee is charged for the entire procedure, including possible readmission fees up to thirty to ninety days after the patient is discharged. Combine this with the fact that today Medicare payments are about 50% of hospital revenues—in five years, they may be as high as 90% of revenues. People I spoke with at the integrated delivery network (IDN) conference are asking a lot of questions. For example:

- How do you know whether previous CER study results remain relevant, particularly if a new product with competing claims has entered the market?
- Do CER findings based on early use of a treatment truly apply to particular clinicians or facilities with extensive experience in more recent refinements?
- What is the source of CER? How is it disseminated? Can findings be extrapolated to a broader range of clinical indications and patients?
- How are supply chain leaders supposed to make decisions on procurement of these technologies, and how do we gather and critique available scientific evidence?
- How do you track and manage the multiple clinical care measures, patient experience measures, and IT measures across a massive population base, and coordinate this with Medicare reimbursement?

These are questions that are causing people to shake their heads. It's going to be an interesting decade for change. Those who are able to grasp and embrace the intricacies and challenges of the healthcare ecosystem will be able to design and leverage supply chain relationships with new solutions, analytical tools, and value-based approaches to these problems. The successful enterprises will focus on patient value, yet continue to drive down costs through strategies such as demand management, collaboration, analytics, and aligned planning. Those who don't will go the way of the dinosaur—so let's get started!

Index

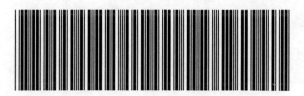